DON'T
BULLSHIT
A BULLSHITTER

JACK HAMMER

Copyright © 2025 by Jack Hammer
All rights reserved.

No portion of this book may be reproduced without written permission from the publisher or author except as permitted by U.S. copyright law.

TABLE OF CONTENTS

Introduction — 1
Why Bullshit Matters — 1
The Universal Truth About Bullshit — 2
The Case for Bullshit — 2
The Problem with Bullshit — 3
Why This Book Exists — 3
A Personal Bullshit Journey — 4
What You'll Learn — 5
Who This Book Is For? — 5
A Quick Disclaimer — 6

CHAPTER 1
What Is Bullshit? — 7
The Many Faces of Bullshit — 7
Lies: The Straight Shooter of Deception — 8
Half-Truths: The Master of Plausibility — 8
Embellishments: Adding Spice to the Story — 9
Outright Nonsense: The Fireworks Finale — 9
Bullshit: A Life Skill in Disguise — 10

CHAPTER 2
The Bullshit Spectrum — 13
Levels of Bullshit — 13

White Lies: Social Comfort Food	13
Performative BS: The Showstopper	14
Malicious BS: The Dark Side	15
Why We Bullshit	15
Interactive Exercise: Spot the BS	16

CHAPTER 3
Case Studies — 19

Pop Culture: BS on the Red Carpet	19
The Influencer's World of Make-Believe	20
Celebrity Tales Taller Than the Hollywood Sign	20
Politics: The Olympics of BS	21
Campaign Promises That Defy Reality	21
The Non-Apology Shuffle	21
Photo Ops and False Relatability	21
Everyday Life: BS in Your Backyard	22
The Friend with "Celebrity Connections"	22
Workplace Shenanigans	22
Social Media Fakery	22
Why We Fall for It	23
Interactive Exercise: Spot the BS	23
Reflections	23

CHAPTER 4
The Tell-Tale Signs — 25

Body Language: When the Body Tells the Truth	25
The Stare That Tries Too Hard	26
Fidget Overload	26
Overcompensating Gestures	26
Over-Explaining: Too Many Words, Not Enough Truth	26
The Avalanche of Unnecessary Details	27
The Imaginary Friend	27
The Never-Ending Monologue	27
Misdirection: The Great Escape	27

The Pivot to Irrelevance	28
Answering a Question with a Question	28
The Dramatic Overreaction	28
Practical Tools for Spotting Bullshit	28
Interactive Exercise: Spot the Bullshitter	29

CHAPTER 5
Classic Phrases — 31

Common Red Flags: The Usual Suspects	31
"Trust me, bro."	31
"Honestly, I wouldn't lie."	32
Hilarious Scenarios: Bullshit in Action	33
Scenario 1: The Financial Guru	33
Scenario 2: The Travel Expert	33
Scenario 3: The Fitness Guru	33
Why These Phrases Work (For a While)	34
Practical Takeaways: Dealing with Classic BS Phrases	34
Interactive Exercise: Spot the BS	34

CHAPTER 6
Bullshit Detectors — 37

Techniques: How to Test a Story Without Breaking a Sweat	37
1. Ask Innocent, Pointed Follow-Ups	37
2. Cross-Check Details	38
3. Play Dumb and Let Them Talk	38
Hilarious Scenarios: Spotting BS in the Wild	39
Scenario 1: The Rock Star Connection	39
Scenario 2: The Social Media Influencer	39
Scenario 3: The Fitness Enthusiast	40
Why These Techniques Work	40
Interactive Exercise: Spot the BS	41

CHAPTER 7
When to Call It Out — 43

To Strike or Let It Slide?	43
Category 1: Harmless BS	43
Category 2: Harmful BS	44
Category 3: Outrageous BS	44
The Art of the Sarcastic Comeback	45
When Sarcasm Isn't the Answer?	46
Reflection Questions: Should You Call It Out?	46
Practical Takeaways: How to Handle BS	46
Interactive Exercise: Strike or Slide?	47
Practical Takeaway	47

CHAPTER 8

Out-Bullshitting a Bullshitter — 49

Techniques: How to Out-BS Like a Pro	49
1. Match Their Confidence	50
2. Use the "Yes, and…" Technique	50
3. Escalate the Absurdity	51
The Bullshit Olympics: Verbal Duels in Action	51
Why Out-BS Works	52
Practical Takeaways: Mastering the Craft	52
Interactive Exercise: Out-BS Practice	53

CHAPTER 9

Levels of Mastery — 55

Level 1: Beginner – Dodging Your Own Pitfalls	55
Level 2: Intermediate – Spotting BS Effortlessly	56
Level 3: Expert – Outsmarting Manipulators with Style	57
Reflection Questions: What's Your Level? Ask yourself	58
Practical Takeaways: Your Path to Mastery	58
Interactive Exercise: What's Your Level?	58

CHAPTER 10

Why Do People Bullshit? — 61

Ego: Look at Me, I'm Awesome	61

Fear: Please Don't Judge Me — 62
Boredom: Let's Make Life Interesting — 63
The Bullshit Trifecta: When Motivations Collide — 63
Reflection Questions: Why Do You BS? — 64

CHAPTER 11
The Psychology of Believability — 67
Confidence: The Power Move — 67
Specificity: Details That Distract — 68
The Echo Effect — 68
Why We Fall for It — 69
How to Spot the Tricks — 69
Practical Takeaways — 70
Reflection Questions — 70

CHAPTER 12
How Society Rewards Bullshit — 73
The Influencer Effect: Selling the Illusion — 73
Corporate Culture: Where Buzzwords Reign Supreme — 74
Why Bullshit Thrives — 75
The Cost of Rewarding Bullshit — 75
How to Resist the Hype — 76
Reflection Questions — 76

CHAPTER 13
When BS is Good — 79
The Noble Bullshitter — 79
Social Glue: BS That Saves Conversations — 79
When BS Saves the Day — 80
The Ethics of Harmless BS — 81
Interactive Practice: Craft Your Noble BS — 82
Practical Tips for Mastering Harmless BS — 82
Reflection Questions — 83

CHAPTER 14
The Ethical Bullshitter's Guide — 85

Rule #1: Never BS About Serious Matters — 85
Rule #2: Make It Fun, Not Harmful — 86
   The Fun vs. Harmful Test — 86
Rule #3: Know When to Stop — 86
The Ethical Bullshitter's Checklist — 87
Examples of Ethical BS in Action — 87
Interactive Exercise: Craft Your Ethical BS — 88
Practical Tips for Ethical BS — 89
Reflection Questions — 89

CHAPTER 15
Leaving a Legacy — 91

Be a Lovable Bullshitter — 91
Stories That Entertain Not Deceive — 91
Unite, Don't Divide — 92
How Bu can Inspire — 93
Crafting a Memorable BS Legacy — 93
Interactive Section: Your Legacy Story — 94
Prompts to Get You Started — 94
Living in a World Full of Nonsense — 94
The Final Takeaway: Be the BS People Love — 95

CHAPTER 16
The BS Detox – Cutting the Crap (Temporarily) — 97

Time to Clear the Air — 97
Why Detox Your BS? — 98
Recognizing Your BS Triggers — 98
The 7-Day BS Detox Plan — 99
   Day 1: Radical Truth — 99
   Day 2: Honest Social Media Post — 100
   Day 3: Admit What You Don't Know — 100

Day 4: Politely Call Out BS	100
Day 5: Own Your Self-Lies	100
Day 6: Say No Without Excuses	101
Day 7: Reflect and Recharge	101
What You'll Gain from the Detox	101
Post-Detox: Returning to Ethical BS	101

CHAPTER 17
Bullshit in Relationships — 105

The Dating Game: Swipe Right for Stories	105
How to Spot Dating BS	106
Family Bullshit: Where Legends Are Born	106
Why BS Flourishes in Relationships	107
Turning BS into an Art Form	108
When to Call Out BS	109
Practical Takeaways	109

CHAPTER 18
Bullshit in the Workplace — 111

The Corporate Language of Nonsense	111
Meetings: The BS Olympics	112
Recognizing the Workplace BS Aficionados	113
Why Workplace BS Persists	113
How to Navigate and Succeed in the BS Zone	114
Play the Game, Don't Be the Game	115

CHAPTER 19
Bullshit in Pop Culture — 117

Hollywood: The Dream Machine	117
Hollywood's Go-To Tropes	118
Instagram: The Influencer's Playground	119
How to Spot the Nonsense	119
Enjoy the Show Without Buying the Fantasy	120

CHAPTER 20
Advanced Bullshit Techniques   123

The Art of Deflection: Dodging Accountability with Style   123
The Complicated Lie: Balancing Intricacy and Plausibility   124
Case Studies: When BS Backfires   125
Mastering Advanced BS: Pro Tips   126
The Art of Storytelling   126

CHAPTER 21
Living a Bullshit-Free Life   129

Escaping the BS Trap: Calling Yourself Out   129
Cutting Through Another People's BS   130
Techniques for Handling Nonsense   130
Radical Honesty: Simplifying Life   131
Living Bullshit-Free: Finding the Balance   131
Bullshit in Technology and the Digital Age   132
    Tech-Savvy BS   132
Navigating Digital Deception   132
Final Thoughts   133

CHAPTER 22
Social Media Smoke and Mirrors   135

The Illusion of Influencers   135
Curated Lifestyles: The Highlight Reel   136
Viral Trends: Absurdity in Action   136
Spotting the Bullshit: A Survival Guide   137
    Inspect the Details   137
    Question Dramatic Claims   137
    Trust Your Instincts   138
Closing Reflection   138

CHAPTER 23
The Clickbait Conundrum   141

Sensational Headlines: The Digital Siren Song   141

Fake News: Lies Disguised as Journalism — 142
How Clickbait and Fake News Exploit Emotions — 143
Strategies for Spotting Credible Sources — 144
Cutting Through the Noise — 145

CHAPTER 24
Battling Algorithmic Bullshit — 147
The Algorithm: Bullshit's Best Friend — 147
Why Outrage Outperforms Reason — 148
The Nonsense Avalanche — 149
How to Outsmart the Algorithm — 150
Reclaiming Your Digital Space — 152

CHAPTER 25
Romantic Bullshit — 155
The Harmless Lies That Keep Love Alive — 155
The Damaging Deceptions That Sink Relationships — 156
Building Trust Without Sacrificing Humor — 157
Navigating Bullshit in the Digital Age — 157
    The Fine Art of Romantic Bullshit — 158

CHAPTER 26
Bullshit at Work — 161
The Game of Office Politics — 162
Co-workers Who Oversell Themselves — 163
Strategies for Managing Workplace Bullshit — 164

CHAPTER 27
The Charismatic Bullshitter — 167
The Art of Storytelling: Inspiring with a Dash of BS — 167
When Charisma Turns to Manipulation — 168
Spotting the Charismatic Bullshitter — 169
Using Charisma for Good: A Guide for Leaders — 170
Charisma with a Conscience — 171

CHAPTER 28
Leading Without Lying — 173

- The Allure of Bullshit in Leadership — 173
- Transparency: The Bedrock of Trust — 174
- Authenticity: Your Leadership Superpower — 175
- Practical Strategies for No-BS Leadership — 176
- The Payoff: Loyalty, Engagement, and Results — 177
  - The No-BS Leadership Manifesto — 177

CHAPTER 29
Following the Bullshitter — 179

- The Fine Line Between Inspiration and Manipulation — 179
- Red Flags: How to Spot Dangerous Bullshit — 180
- When (and How) to Call Out Bullshit — 181
- How to Follow a Bullshitter Without Losing Your Mind — 182
- Thriving Despite the Bullshit — 183

CHAPTER 30
Hollywood Bullshit — 185

- The "Based on a True Story" Trap — 185
- Unrealistic Character Arcs: From Zero to Hero in 90 Minutes — 186
  - Why We Love to Suspend Disbelief — 187
  - When Bullshit Enhances Storytelling — 188
- Embracing Hollywood's Nonsense — 189
- Key Examples of Hollywood Nonsense — 189

CHAPTER 31
Marketing Myths — 191

- The Tall Tales of Ad Campaigns — 191
- Why We Fall for the Nonsense — 192
- Spotting the Marketing Myths — 193
  - Read the Fine Print — 193
  - Question the Numbers — 193
  - Identify the Emotional Hook — 194

Do Your Research	194
Embracing Humor and Skepticism	194
Why We Keep Buying (and That's Okay)	194
Marketing Myths as Entertainment	195
Summary	195

CHAPTER 32
Bullshit and the Post-Truth Era — 197

Feelings Over Facts: The Rise of Emotional Truth	197
The Echo Chamber Effect	198
Why Perception Outweighs Reality	199
Promoting Truth in a Post-Truth World	200
The Final BS Breakdown	201
The Grand Takeaway	203

INTRODUCTION

WHY BULLSHIT MATTERS

Bullshit doesn't just walk; it takes center stage, does a cartwheel, and sticks the landing. You've probably heard someone say, "Bullshit walks and money talks." It's a phrase that typically comes from an overly confident uncle at Thanksgiving or that one friend who still uses words like "the bee's knees." But let's be honest: bullshit doesn't just walk. It sprints marathons, climbs mountains, and infiltrates every corner of our lives.

Think about it. Bullshit is everywhere in your office meetings, on your social media feeds, in politics, and at your cousin's wedding, where the groom claimed he invented a "portable microwave" (spoiler: it's called a lunchbox). It's as unavoidable as a cold in flu season.

But what is bullshit exactly? Is it lying? Not always. Is it an exaggeration? Sometimes. Is it storytelling with a little too much creative license? Absolutely. Bullshit is the art of dancing around the truth, throwing in just enough believable detail to make everyone nod along, even if, deep down, they know you're full of it.

And guess what? Everyone does it. Yes, even you.

THE UNIVERSAL TRUTH ABOUT BULLSHIT

Here's a little secret: nobody is entirely immune to bullshit. Some of us are seasoned professionals charming our way through awkward parties with "interesting" stories about hiking adventures we never actually took. Others are amateurs, dabbling in white lies like "I'm five minutes away" when you're still in pajamas.

Then, there are the unknowing victims. You're at a company meeting, nodding along as Steve from marketing says, "Our customer engagement is up 700%," even though you've never met a single "customer." Or maybe you've politely listened to your dad's tale about that once he almost went pro in baseball despite zero photographic evidence and a beer belly suggesting otherwise.

You might think, not me. I'm a bullshit ninja. I see through everything. Oh, really? So, you've never clicked on a headline like "Doctors Hate This Simple Trick" or fallen for your coworker's "gluten intolerance" just to watch them inhale a croissant on a Tuesday?

Yeah. That's what I thought.

THE CASE FOR BULLSHIT

Bullshit gets a bad rap, and sure, some of it deserves the stink eye. Malicious bullshit scams, misinformation, MLM pitches can wreak havoc. But not all bullshit is created equal. In fact, some of it is downright essential.

Think of bullshit as the social duct tape holding humanity together. It keeps awkward conversations from crashing and burning ("Oh, your cat runs an Instagram account? Fascinating!"). It spices up dull moments ("Did I ever tell you about the time I arm-wrestled The Rock?"). And let's not forget its role in navigating life's minefields, like job interviews and first dates.

Consider this: How often have you told a harmless white lie to keep the peace? Or exaggerated a story to make your friends laugh? Or nodded along in a meeting when you had no clue what was happening? That's not lying. That's social lubrication. Bullshit is what makes us human, and sometimes, it's what makes us tolerable.

THE PROBLEM WITH BULLSHIT

Of course, bullshit isn't all fun and games. It has a dark side. Weaponized bullshit scams, propaganda, and your aunt's "miracle diet pills" can destroy trust, damage relationships, and ruin entire elections. (Yeah, I'm going there. Buckle up for Chapter 4.)

The challenge is figuring out when bullshit is harmless and when it's downright toxic. This book will help you develop the skills to navigate bullshit like a pro: knowing when to call it out, when to let it slide, and when to use it to your advantage ethically, of course. (Mostly.)

WHY THIS BOOK EXISTS

You might be thinking, why write a whole book about bullshit? Isn't it just part of life, like Mondays or slow Wi-Fi? Sure, but here's the problem: most people don't really understand bullshit. They either fall for it too quickly, get outraged by it unnecessarily, or wield it recklessly like a toddler with a permanent marker.

That's where this book comes in. Don't Bullshit a Bullshitter isn't just a guide; it's a survival manual. It's your compass in a world where half-truths and tall tales are the norm. By the end of this book, you'll be able to spot bullshit from a mile away, dodge it with finesse, and even deploy it responsibly when the situation calls for it.

Here's what we'll cover:

- The Anatomy of Bullshit: What it is, why we do it, and how it works. Spotting the Bullshitter: How to recognize the red flags and protect yourself from getting duped.
- Mastering the Bullshit Arts: Ethical bullshit strategies for work, relationships, and social situations.
- The Social Science of Bullshit: Why it's an inevitable part of human interaction (and what it says about us).
- When Bullshit Saves the Day: Real-life stories where bullshit turned out to be a hero in disguise.

A PERSONAL BULLSHIT JOURNEY

Let me tell you about Brian, my college buddy. Brian could bullshit his way out of anything. Once, while completely hungover, he convinced our professor that his computer had been hacked by a guy named "Abe" to explain why he hadn't turned in his assignment. Not only did Brian get an extension, but the professor actually apologized for the inconvenience.

At first, I was horrified. But then I realized Brian wasn't just lying; he was telling a story, and people love stories. Even when they're ridiculous. Especially when they're ridiculous.

That's when I started paying attention to the role bullshit plays in our lives. It's not just about deception but connection, creativity, and, sometimes, survival. And if you learn to master it, you can handle just about anything life throws your way.

WHAT YOU'LL LEARN

By the end of this book, you'll have:

- A bullshit radar so finely tuned you could spot a scam email from outer space.
- The confidence to call out bullshit when necessary and the wisdom to let it slide when it's not worth it.
- The skills to bullshit responsibly adding just enough flair to charm your way through life.
- A deeper understanding of why bullshit is both a curse and a gift.

WHO THIS BOOK IS FOR?

This book is for anyone who's ever fallen for a fake excuse, endured a jargon-filled work meeting, or nodded along to a story that felt more fiction than fact. It's for the skeptics who want sharper tools and the storytellers who want better craft. Whether you're a seasoned bullshitter, a recovering victim, or just trying to survive a world of nonsense, this book is for you.

A QUICK DISCLAIMER

Let's clarify: this isn't a guide for becoming a manipulative jerk. Ethical bullshit is about creativity and charm, not exploitation. If you're here to learn how to scam people, kindly exit stage left and maybe reconsider your life choices.

Bullshit is everywhere, and it's not going anywhere. The question is: will you let it control you, or will you learn to prevent it? By the end of this book, you'll laugh, you'll learn, and you'll never get bullshitted again.

CHAPTER 1

WHAT IS BULLSHIT?

Bullshit, like glitter at a craft fair, is everywhere, and once it sticks, it's nearly impossible to shake off. It infiltrates your inbox with "guaranteed weight loss in 7 days" promises, clogs your Instagram feed with influencers surviving on "gratitude and match lattes," and shows up in your relationships when your friend claims they're "five minutes away" while still picking out socks. But before we go further, let's break down what this glittery nonsense really is.

Bullshit isn't just a fib, nor is it a full-blown fabrication. It's a playful mix of creativity and audacity. Picture lying and storytelling, having a child, and that child abandoning a corporate job to live as a bohemian poet. That's bullshit. It takes dull truths, sprinkles them with sequins, and turns them into something too captivating to ignore, even if you suspect it's not entirely real.

THE MANY FACES OF BULLSHIT

Bullshit's charm lies in its adaptability. It ranges from harmless little tweaks, like claiming you "love hiking" even though your last trek ended with bug spray in your eyes, to dangerous cons, like Ponzi schemes wrapped in slick marketing. Whether it entertains, deceives, or gets us out of awkward moments, bullshit thrives because, deep down, we want it to. After all, who wouldn't enjoy a world where someone's cousin wrestled a bear in Alaska?

LIES: THE STRAIGHT SHOOTER OF DECEPTION

Lies are direct and deliberate, like when someone says, "I didn't eat your last slice of pizza," even as the evidence (and crumbs) say otherwise. Lies are efficient, but they lack the flair of great bullshit. They're like fast food: quick, straightforward, and ultimately unsatisfying.

While lies can save you in a pinch, ``like claiming "I'm stuck in traffic" to avoid an awkward meeting, they're risky. Lies can't pivot or charm out of exposure; the game's over once caught. Bullshit, by contrast, thrives in ambiguity and creativity, making it the Swiss Army knife of deception.

HALF-TRUTHS: THE MASTER OF PLAUSIBILITY

Half-truths are the sweet spot between fact and fiction. They're grounded enough in reality to be believable but still have wiggle room for exaggeration. For when, a coworker claims, "I've been swamped with emails all day," while spending most of their time Googling "how to look busy at work." Half-truths thrive in the gray area, where creativity meets plausibility.

The brilliance of half-truths is their plausible deniability. If caught, you can always backtrack with a technicality like, "Well, technically..." But beware: half-truths can be a slippery slope. The habit of sprinkling fiction into your facts can snowball into wild claims like, "I almost got cast in a Marvel movie" because a barista complimented your cheekbones.

EMBELLISHMENTS: ADDING SPICE TO THE STORY

If lies are plain oatmeal, embellishments are the cinnamon and sugar that make them palatable. They shush up dull truths into stories worth sharing. "I caught a fish" becomes "I caught a fish so massive it could've been on Shark Week." These harmless exaggerations add charm and excitement to conversations.

The key to embellishments is moderation. A touch of creative flair can turn a bland anecdote into a crowd-pleaser. But overdo it, and you veer into Cringe Territory, where "I took a scenic hike" becomes "I discovered an uncharted trail system." Nobody wants to be the try-hard storyteller who derails game night.

OUTRIGHT NONSENSE: THE FIREWORKS FINALE

Outright nonsense is bullshit in its boldest form, where logic takes a backseat. It's the coworker who insists they invented Post-it Notes or the friend who swears they saw Bigfoot but conveniently forgot their phone. This level of bullshit doesn't care about plausibility; it's all about spectacle.

The magic of outright nonsense lies in its audacity. It demands confidence and charisma to pull off. It can captivate an audience eager to believe in a world where the impossible happens. But tread carefully without charm and conviction; you're just the person trying to pass off your house cat as a tiger named Sparky.

BULLSHIT: A LIFE SKILL IN DISGUISE

Bullshit, in all its forms, is part of life. From subtle half-truths to jaw-dropping nonsense, it's woven into human interaction. The trick isn't to avoid it but to recognize it, appreciate its craft, and, when necessary, use it with purpose.

In the kingdom of bullshit, confidence reigns supreme. So, the next time someone tells you they "met Beyoncé at a gas station" or "ran a marathon," just smile, nod, and enjoy the performance. After all, even in its most exaggerated forms, bullshit has a way of keeping life interesting.

Now that you know what bullshit looks like, let's dive deeper into why we love it so much and why it's here to stay. Bullshit is a universal phenomenon, blending truth, creativity, and audacity to entertain, impress, or smooth over awkward moments.

Unlike lies, which are deliberate and straightforward, bullshit is more artful, a mix of embellishment and half-truths designed to captivate or distract. It thrives daily, from exaggerated Instagram posts and marketing buzzwords to your coworker's insistence that they invented Post-it Notes. Whether it's a harmless fib or a jaw-dropping tale, bullshit's charm lies in its adaptability and its ability to transform the mundane into something memorable.

This chapter breaks down the many faces of bullshit. Lies are efficient but lack the flair of half-truths, which add just enough plausibility to keep things believable. Embellishments spice up dull anecdotes, turning "I caught a fish" into "I caught a fish big enough for

Shark Week." At the same time, outright nonsense demands audacity, like claiming you saw Bigfoot but forgot your phone.

Bullshit, when wielded with confidence and moderation, isn't just deception. It's a life skill that makes conversations lively and interactions more engaging. Recognizing its forms allows you to appreciate its craft, navigate its presence, and use it responsibly to add sparkle without crossing into manipulation.

CHAPTER 2

THE BULLSHIT SPECTRUM

Bullshit isn't a one-size-fits-all phenomenon. It spans a spectrum from harmless white lies to malicious deception that makes you question humanity (and your bank account balance). Think of it as a rainbow of nonsense, except the end doesn't hold a pot of gold. Instead, it's more likely to lead to a raised eyebrow or a desperate call to customer service.

Understanding this spectrum equips you with a finely tuned BS radar. Some bullshit deserves no more than a polite nod and a knowing smile. Other times, it's the kind that lands you Googling "how to report a scam."

LEVELS OF BULLSHIT

Let's explore the spectrum, starting with the lightest, most innocent fibs and ending with the heavyweight champions of deception.

WHITE LIES: SOCIAL COMFORT FOOD

White lies are the fluffiest nonsense on the spectrum of tiny fibs designed to make social interactions smoother. You've told a few today.

"I love your haircut!" (You don't.) "I'll be there on time!" (You won't.) "Your baby is adorable!" (Questionable.)

These fibs are the bubble wrap of human interaction, cushioning awkwardness and protecting feelings. Without them, life would be a series of brutal truths like, "Your cookies taste like sadness." The charm of white lies is their harmlessness. They add just enough seasoning to conversations without tipping into dishonesty overload.

That said, overusing white lies can backfire. When everything you say feels prepackaged, people might doubt your sincerity. Use them sparingly, like a sprinkle of salt, not the entire shaker.

PERFORMATIVE BS: THE SHOWSTOPPER

Performative BS is where things get dramatic. It's not just a fib; it's a full-on production. Designed to dazzle, this nonsense thrives in social media feeds, party anecdotes, or family gatherings. These tales start with a shred of truth and balloon into: "And then I saved a busload of orphans with nothing but my determination and a Swiss Army knife."

The problem? Performative BS rarely holds up under scrutiny. It's the "Wait, didn't you say you're afraid of heights? How did you skydive into a burning building?" kind of storytelling. The key to identifying this level is its over-the-top flair. If it sounds like a rejected plot from an action movie, it's probably BS.

Still, it's entertaining. Performative BS may be nonsense, but it's the kind you can appreciate for its creativity until the details unravel.

MALICIOUS BS: THE DARK SIDE

At the far end of the spectrum lies malicious BS designed to deceive, exploit, or harm. This is where bullshit takes a sinister turn. Think scam emails promising millions if you share your bank details or Ponzi schemes that bleed you dry while promising "guaranteed" returns.

What sets malicious BS apart is intent. White lies aim to protect feelings; malicious BS aims to manipulate. It's the coworker hyping a project as "career-defining" while plotting their exit, leaving you to clean up the mess. Unlike performative BS, this isn't for laughs; it's for personal gain at someone else's expense.

The silver lining? Few things are as satisfying as exposing malicious BS. Watching a scammer squirm when their lies collapse is pure gold. Don't expect them to admit defeat; doubling down is often their go-to move.

WHY WE BULLSHIT

Here's the kicker: nobody thinks of themselves as a bullshitter. Everyone has a reason, a justification for their nonsense. Let's explore the top hits:

- "It's for their own good." Parents telling kids, "If you swallow gum, it'll stay in your stomach for seven years," use this defense. It's not true, but it's effective.
- "It's not really lying." This gray-area excuse involves "creative phrasing." For instance, "VP of Coffee Acquisition" is a fancy way of saying "Starbucks barista."

- "It makes the story better." Losing your wallet becomes an epic tale of surviving without ID, cash, or dignity in a foreign country. Because, let's face it, embellishment makes everything more fun.

These justifications remind us that, at its core, bullshit often stems from a desire to make life a little more bearable or at least more interesting.

INTERACTIVE EXERCISE: SPOT THE BS

Put your BS radar to the test. Here are some statements. Decide where they fall on the spectrum: white lies, performative BS, or malicious nonsense.

"I didn't eat your leftovers, I swear!"

"I once ran a marathon in under three hours. Didn't even train for it!"

"This investment opportunity is 100% risk-free. Just send $500 to my PayPal."

Answers:
- White Lie
- Performative BS
- Malicious BS

If you got these rights, congrats! You're officially on your way to becoming a certified bullshit detective. Remember this framework the next time someone swears they've "discovered the procrastination cure."

Bullshit comes in all shapes and sizes, but it always leaves clues. From harmless fibs to jaw-dropping scams, recognizing where nonsense falls on the spectrum is the first step to navigating it. The next time someone claims, "This smoothie changed my life," smile, nod, and quietly ask yourself: Where does this fall on the Bullshit Spectrum?

Then, decide if it's worth challenging or if it's better to just let it glitter in the background.

The Bullshit Spectrum explores the wide range of nonsense we encounter daily, from harmless white lies to malicious deception. White lies act as social lubricants at the gentlest end, smoothing awkward moments and sparing feelings with minor fibs like complimenting a questionable haircut or pretending to love someone's overcooked dinner.

Moving up the spectrum, performative BS adds drama and flair, turning mundane truths into elaborate productions meant to impress or entertain, such as tales of heroics that rival blockbuster movies.

At its darkest, malicious BS emerges as deceit designed to harm or exploit, such as scams or manipulative schemes aimed at personal gain at someone else's expense.

Understanding why people bullshit is equally revealing. Often, it stems from good intentions or a desire to make life more entertaining. Parents might stretch the truth for "their own good." In contrast, others embellish to enhance storytelling or reframe their lives more impressively.

However, not all BS is harmless, and recognizing where it falls on the spectrum is key to navigating it wisely. Whether it's a coworker hyping their role with creative job titles or a scammer promising a risk-free investment, knowing how to spot red flags and motives helps you engage with or avoid the nonsense effectively.

CHAPTER 3

CASE STUDIES

By now, you're probably thinking, okay, I get it; bullshit is everywhere. But what does it actually look like in action? Glad you asked. Welcome to the Bullshit Hall of Fame, where we analyze the most iconic nonsense from pop culture, politics, and everyday life. This guided tour of curated absurdity will sharpen your BS radar while delivering a few laughs.

Why case studies? Because bullshit isn't always easy to spot. Sometimes, it's subtle, like a politician "misspeaking," but other times, it's hilariously outrageous like an influencer claiming they're "just like you" while lounging on a yacht. You'll learn to navigate a nonsense-filled world by dissecting these examples and maybe even enjoy the spectacle.

POP CULTURE: BS ON THE RED CARPET

If there's a mecca for bullshit, it's pop culture. Celebrities and influencers craft images that are so curated that they make your uncle's fishing stories look credible. Hollywood runs on fantasy, and its stars have mastered spinning magic into their public personas.

THE INFLUENCER'S WORLD OF MAKE-BELIEVE

Influencers specialize in selling an illusion. That perfectly casual morning routine they post? It probably required a professional photographer, multiple outfit changes, and a team of assistants to hold the lighting reflector. Their caption, "Just a chill morning," means: "I spent two hours curating this shot so you'll think my life is perfect."

Exaggeration is their bread and butter. "This serum is a game-changer," they gush, omitting that they were paid $10,000 to promote it and haven't even used it. Then there's the ultimate move: the "relatable" post. "Just me, living my best life!" they write, sipping champagne in a penthouse overlooking Paris. Relatable? Sure, if your life includes a six-figure brand deal and a personal assistant.

CELEBRITY TALES TALLER THAN THE HOLLYWOOD SIGN

Celebrities aren't far behind. Take the actor who insists they did "90% of their stunts." Translation: they walked briskly down a hallway while their stunt double leaped out of a helicopter. Then there are awards speeches: "This one's for the fans!" Sure, but the $20 million paycheck probably didn't hurt.

Endorsements are another goldmine of nonsense. Does your favorite pop star really drink that diet soda they're selling? Doubtful. More likely, they're sipping imported glacier water while cashing the endorsement check.

POLITICS: THE OLYMPICS OF BS

Pop culture may provide the glitter, but politics brings the heavyweight competition. Campaign season, in particular, is a masterclass in stretching the truth until it snaps.

CAMPAIGN PROMISES THAT DEFY REALITY

"I'll create 10 million new jobs!" sounds incredible until you dig deeper and realize those jobs might involve selling leggings in a multilevel marketing scheme. Politicians excel at making grand promises with zero specifics, relying on the headline to stick just long enough to secure votes.

THE NON-APOLOGY SHUFFLE

Then there's the non-apology: "I'm sorry if anyone was offended." Translation: "I don't think I did anything wrong, but my PR team said I had to say this." It's a political tradition saying everything and nothing all at once.

PHOTO OPS AND FALSE RELATABILITY

Politicians love a good photo op. Whether posing with a baby, a firefighter, or a farmer, the goal is the same: to appear relatable. Holding a baby doesn't qualify you to fix the economy, but it looks good on a campaign poster. Bonus points if the baby cries. It's a perfect metaphor for the voter's dashed hopes.

EVERYDAY LIFE: BS IN YOUR BACKYARD

Of course, you don't need Hollywood or Capitol Hill to find bullshit. It's alive and well in everyday life.

THE FRIEND WITH "CELEBRITY CONNECTIONS"

We all know someone who claims, "I met Beyoncé in an elevator. She smiled at me!" Sure, Jan. Beyoncé definitely rides elevators and makes small talk with strangers. More likely, your friend mistook someone with great hair for Queen Bey and ran with it.

WORKPLACE SHENANIGANS

Workplace BS deserves its own award category. The coworker claims, "I thrive under pressure," only to vanish during crunch time. Or the manager who says, "We're all a family here," just before asking you to work unpaid overtime. And job titles? "Chief Happiness Officer" is just HR with a whimsical twist, and "Data Wizard" means you're good with Excel.

SOCIAL MEDIA FAKERY

Social media is the epicenter of everyday nonsense. Carefully curated vacation photos and inspirational quotes create a nonstop illusion of perfect lives. No, Karen, your "peaceful morning meditation" wasn't peaceful; you just cropped out the toddler throwing cereal at the dog.

WHY WE FALL FOR IT

Here's the thing: we want to believe the bullshit. We'd love to live in a world where celebrities do stunts, politicians keep their promises, and Beyoncé smiles at strangers. Bullshit sells us comfort, even when it's far from the truth.

There's also laziness at play. Fact-checking takes effort, and scrolling past is more effortless. Bullshit thrives on our willingness to nod and move on.

INTERACTIVE EXERCISE: SPOT THE BS

Let's test your BS radar. Match the statement to its corresponding level of nonsense:

"This face cream made me look 10 years younger!"

"If elected, I'll fix the economy in six months."

"I ran into Beyoncé at Target. We bonded over candles."

Answers:

Pop Culture BS (The cream probably made them shinier, not younger.)

Political BS (Fixing the economy? Sure.)

Everyday BS (Beyoncé doesn't shop for candles, but she has assistants for that)

REFLECTIONS

Bullshit is everywhere, from influencers to politicians to your neighbor who swears they "almost made it on The Voice." The trick isn't to eliminate it (impossible) but to spot it, laugh at it, and decide when to call it out.

Because here's the reality: you can't stop people from bullshitting, but you can prevent yourself from falling for it. So, the next time someone brags about their "life-changing serum" or claims they "met Beyoncé at Target," just smile, nod, and enjoy the show. After all, even the most outrageous nonsense makes life a little more entertaining.

Bullshit infiltrates every corner of life, from the glitz of pop culture to the chaos of politics and the absurdity of everyday interactions. In pop culture, influencers and celebrities excel at creating illusions.

Influencers curate seemingly effortless perfection with staged "relatable" posts. At the same time, celebrities embellish stories, like doing "90% of their stunts," to maintain their star power. These fabrications entertain, but they're often as believable as the action sequences in Hollywood blockbusters. Whether it's a "game-changing" serum or an "authentic" connection to fans, pop culture BS thrives because we're willing to suspend disbelief for a taste of fantasy.

Politics brings a heavyweight flair to BS with grandiose campaign promises, hollow non-apologies, and staged photo ops. Voters often fall for the spectacle, whether the politician claiming to fix the economy in record time or smiling with a baby to appear relatable.

Everyday life is no stranger to nonsense: friends boasting celebrity connections, coworkers with inflated resumes, and social media profiles projecting impossibly perfect lives. While it's tempting to fall for these fabrications, spotting and laughing at the absurdity of these tales is the key to navigating the noise without getting caught up in it.

CHAPTER 4

THE TELL-TALE SIGNS

Let's get one thing straight: bullshitters aren't as subtle as they like to believe. They might fancy themselves as master manipulators, but they're as apparent as a toddler hiding under a blanket, convinced no one can see them. Spotting their nonsense is easy if you know what to look for.

Bullshitters rely on your willingness to buy into their stories. Their words might sound smooth, but their actions, body language, and overcompensation often betray them. This chapter is your cheat sheet for identifying their tricks. We'll break it down into three categories: body language, over-explaining, and misdirection.

BODY LANGUAGE: WHEN THE BODY TELLS THE TRUTH

Words can lie, but the body rarely cooperates. A bullshitter's physical cues often contradict their story, making body language one of the easiest ways to spot deception.

THE STARE THAT TRIES TOO HARD

You've seen the uncomfortably intense eye contact that feels more like a hostage situation than a conversation. This is the "Believe me or else" stare, where they lock eyes, unblinking, as they weave their tale. "Oh yeah, I know Elon Musk. We met at this exclusive retreat in the Maldives," they'll say, pupils dilated from sheer panic masked as confidence.

Pro Tip: They're probably bluffing if their eye contact feels forced or overly intense.

FIDGET OVERLOAD

On the flip side, some bullshitters can't stay still. Their hands become overly expressive, their feet shuffle toward the nearest exit, and their gestures grow exaggerated. "The presentation? Oh, nailed it! Everyone clapped!" they'll claim, while their drumming fingers suggest otherwise.

OVERCOMPENSATING GESTURES

For some, lying isn't just verbal; it's a performance. "The waves were THIS high when I was surfing in Hawaii!" they'll exclaim, flailing their arms like an audition for a disaster movie. The rule is simple: the bigger the gesture, the bigger the lie.

OVER-EXPLAINING: TOO MANY WORDS, NOT ENOUGH TRUTH

If their body language doesn't give them away, their words will. Bullshitters rarely stick to the basics; instead, they overwhelm you with irrelevant details to sound credible.

THE AVALANCHE OF UNNECESSARY DETAILS

Ask a simple question, "Did you finish the report?" and prepare for a long-winded saga about their morning routine, the traffic they encountered, and their dog's dental emergency. Genuine people stick to the facts. Bullshitters, on the other hand, mistake verbosity for believability.

THE IMAGINARY FRIEND

Every bullshitter has a go-to "friend" who conveniently lends credibility to their story. "Oh, I know someone in the FBI whose name's Steve." Because every top-secret agent introduces themselves casually at parties, right? When pressed for details, their story often unravels into vague nonsense.

Tip: Ask for specifics. If "Steve" suddenly becomes an enigma, you've spotted the lie.

THE NEVER-ENDING MONOLOGUE

Bullshitters rarely know when to quit. What starts as a simple anecdote snowballs into an epic of tangents and callbacks? Let them keep talking. The longer they ramble, the more likely they will trip over their lies.

MISDIRECTION: THE GREAT ESCAPE

When cornered, bullshitters rely on distraction. Misdirection is their escape hatch, designed to steer the conversation away from their lie and into safer territory.

THE PIVOT TO IRRELEVANCE

You ask directly, "Did you close that deal?" they're suddenly discussing their weekend plans. "Oh, did I tell you I started paddle boarding?" It's a classic deflection tactic to make you forget the original question.

Pro Tip: Don't let them off the hook. Bring the conversation back to the topic at hand.

ANSWERING A QUESTION WITH A QUESTION

"Did you finish the report?" morphs into, "Why do you always doubt me?" Suddenly, you're the one on the defensive while they dodge accountability. Stay calm and persistent: "I'm not doubting you, just confirming." Watch their confidence crumble.

THE DRAMATIC OVERREACTION

When all else fails, bullshitters go whole drama. "Wow, I can't believe you'd even ask me that!" they'll exclaim, clutching their metaphorical pearls. This exaggerated offense is meant to guilt you into dropping the subject. Don't fall for it. Genuine people don't overreact to simple questions.

PRACTICAL TOOLS FOR SPOTTING BULLSHIT

Now that you know the signs, here are three quick tips to sharpen your BS radar:

- Trust Your Gut: If their story feels off, it probably is.
- Ask Questions: Follow-ups make lies harder to maintain.
- Stay Focused: Don't let them distract you with tangents or guilt trips.

INTERACTIVE EXERCISE: SPOT THE BULLSHITTER

Let's practice. Identify the tell-tale signs of BS in these scenarios:

Your coworker claims they "work best under pressure" but constantly miss deadlines.

A friend says they saw a ghost but can't explain why their phone "mysteriously" stopped working when they tried to take a photo.

Someone brags about their VIP invite to a celebrity event but dodges every question.

Answers:

Over-Explaining. (Deadlines don't lie; bullshitters do.)

Misdirection. (Ghosts or technical glitches? You decide.)

The Stare and Pivot. (VIP invite? More like a Very Imaginary Party.)

Spotting a bullshitter is like watching a bad magician. They're convinced they're pulling off the trick of the century, but you've already seen the rabbit poking out of the hat. So, the next time someone starts weaving an epic tale of their surfing skills, FBI connections, or mysteriously malfunctioning ghost cameras, sit back, enjoy the show, and remember: the art of catching bullshit is just as entertaining as the art of creating it.

Bullshitters often think they're masters of deception, but their actions and words frequently betray them. This chapter explores the key signs of nonsense in action, focusing on body language, over-explaining, and misdirection.

Bullshitters' physical cues often contradict their words, from exaggerated gestures and fidgeting to forced, intense eye contact that screams desperation rather than confidence.

Over-explaining is another hallmark, as bullshitters overwhelm conversations with irrelevant details, imaginary friends, and endless monologues, mistaking verbosity for credibility.

Meanwhile, misdirection becomes their escape route, pivoting to unrelated topics or using dramatic overreactions to deflect scrutiny and guilt their audience into submission.

Recognizing these behaviors is crucial to sharpening your BS radar. Practical tools include trusting your instincts, asking direct follow-up questions, and staying focused on the topic to avoid distractions from coworkers bragging about "thriving under pressure" while missing deadlines to friends spinning ghost stories with conveniently failing cameras; spotting these tell-tale signs can turn you into a skilled detector of nonsense. The key is to stay curious, persistent, and entertained by the spectacle, as catching BS is often as amusing as the act itself.

CHAPTER 5

CLASSIC PHRASES

You've heard them before, those clichéd lines that practically come with their own flashing neon sign, Warning: Bullshit Ahead! Phrases like "Trust me, bro" or "Honestly, I wouldn't lie" aren't just subtle hints; they're alarm bells. These verbal safety nets are what bullshitters grab onto when their stories start to fall apart. Recognizing them is your key to detecting nonsense and staying a step ahead.

In this chapter, we'll dissect these classic bullshitter phrases: what they mean, why they're so common, and how to dismantle them effortlessly. By the end, you'll have the confidence to call out BS or at least enjoy watching the bullshitter squirm.

COMMON RED FLAGS: THE USUAL SUSPECTS

"TRUST ME, BRO."

This is the holy grail of bullshitter phrases confident, casual, and void of any actual substance. When someone says, "Trust me, bro," they're really saying, I have no evidence, no plan, and no idea what I'm doing, but I'd like you to pretend I do.

Picture this: Your friend offers to fix your dishwasher. "Trust me, bro, it's just a loose wire." Fast forward an hour, and your kitchen looks like a water park, complete with your friend Googling how to repair dishwashers for dummies.

Pro Tip: The more someone insists you trust them, the less you should. Trust professionals, not overconfident amateurs.

"HONESTLY, I WOULDN'T LIE."

"Honestly" should be a red flag, not a reassurance. This phrase is the verbal equivalent of a magician saying, "I swear, there's no rabbit in this hat," seconds before pulling out a rabbit.

Here's how it works: Your coworker arrives late, claiming, "Honestly, traffic was insane this morning." Translation: I hit snooze three times and swung by Starbucks. Or your friend slurs, "Honestly, I'm not drunk," after two tequila shots. Sure, Jan.

Key Insight: Honest people don't feel the need to advertise their honesty. If they're selling it, there's probably a reason.

"Everyone knows..."

Bullshitters love this one because it sidesteps facts and makes their claims seem like common knowledge. It's their shortcut to sounding informed without having to back it up.

Example: "Everyone knows putting your phone in the freezer makes it charge faster." Really? Who's your neighbor's cat?

Pro Tip: Challenge this by asking, "Who exactly is 'everyone'?" Watching their confidence deflate is always worth it.

HILARIOUS SCENARIOS: BULLSHIT IN ACTION

Now that we've covered the basics, let's take these classic phrases into action.

SCENARIO 1: THE FINANCIAL GURU

Friend: "Trust me, bro, crypto is the future. You need to invest in this coin - it's exploding!"

You: "Which coin?"

Friend: "Uh... I forget the name, but honestly, I wouldn't lie."

Translation: Your friend got this "hot tip" from a YouTube comment section.

SCENARIO 2: THE TRAVEL EXPERT

Coworker: "I've been to Bali three times. Everyone knows it's the best place to find yourself."

You: "Oh, cool! What's your favorite spot there?"

Coworker: "Uh... I can't remember, but trust me, bro, it was life changing."

Translation: They've never been to Bali but follow five Bali-themed Instagram accounts.

SCENARIO 3: THE FITNESS GURU

Friend: "Honestly, you don't even need to work out. Everyone knows this supplement melts fat while you sleep."

You: "What's the supplement called?"

Friend: "Oh, I forget the name, but trust me, bro, it works."

Translation: The "supplement" is probably caffeine pills or a scam.

WHY THESE PHRASES WORK (FOR A WHILE)

These phrases work because they sound casual and confident, making you less likely to question them. They're designed to lull you into a false sense of agreement. The moment you challenge their claims, however, the whole facade crumbles.

The trick? Don't take these phrases at face value. Ask questions, stay calm, and watch the bullshitter's confidence unravel.

PRACTICAL TAKEAWAYS: DEALING WITH CLASSIC BS PHRASES

- Ask for Details: Bullshitters hate specifics. The more you press for details, the more likely they will trip themselves up.
- Stay Unshaken: Confidence isn't the same as truth. Don't let their bravado intimidate you.
- Play Along (For Fun): Sometimes, letting a bullshitter dig their own hole is the most entertaining option.

INTERACTIVE EXERCISE: SPOT THE BS

Test your BS radar. Can you identify the classic phrases in these scenarios?

- "Honestly, I wouldn't lie, I met Beyoncé at Coachella."

- "Trust me, bro, this car is a steal. Everyone knows these models last forever."
- "Everyone knows aliens built the pyramids. It's just common sense."

Answers:

"Honestly, I wouldn't lie" = They're lying.

"Trust me, bro" = Don't trust them.

"Everyone knows" = Nobody knows.

Classic bullshit phrases are like cheap cologne overused, overwhelming, and impossible to ignore. But now, you're equipped to sniff them out with the precision of a trained bloodhound. The next time someone tosses out, "Trust me, bro," or "Honestly, I wouldn't lie," just smile, ask a pointed question, and enjoy watching them try to wriggle their way out.

Remember: the more confident the delivery, the less credible the claim. And when all else fails, channel your inner detective and ask the magic question: "Who exactly is everyone?"

Bullshitters often lean on clichéd phrases that scream, Warning: Nonsense Ahead! These classic lines, such as "Trust me, bro," "Honestly, I wouldn't lie," or "Everyone knows," serve as verbal crutches to prop up shaky stories. Designed to sound confident and authoritative, they are often the first sign that someone's claim lacks substance. "Trust me, bro" is the hallmark of overconfidence, masking ignorance. At the same time, "Honestly, I wouldn't lie" suggests they're trying too hard to sell their honesty. Similarly, "Everyone knows" sidesteps facts by invoking an imaginary consensus, leaving their claims unchallenged—until you ask, "Who exactly is everyone?"

These phrases work temporarily because they rely on casual charm and bravado to lull listeners into agreement. However, pressing for specifics quickly unravels the façade, revealing the lack of truth beneath the confident exterior.

To deal with classic BS, ask detailed questions, remain calm, and enjoy the unraveling as they struggle to maintain their story. Whether you call them out or play along for amusement, understanding these telltale phrases ensures you'll never fall for them again. When someone throws out one of these lines, smile and ask the ultimate BS buster: "Can you back that up?"

CHAPTER 6

BULLSHIT DETECTORS

You know the feeling. You're halfway through someone's story when that little voice in your head whispers, this can't possibly be true. Maybe it's your coworker claiming they "single-handedly saved the company" or your cousin insisting they "almost got cast in a Marvel movie." Your BS radar starts pinging like a metal detector over a landfill of tall tales.

Welcome to Bullshit Detectors 101: your guide to calling out nonsense without breaking a sweat or burning bridges. In this chapter, you'll learn subtle yet effective techniques to test tall tales, ask the right questions, and enjoy watching the house of cards fall, all while keeping the interaction fun and lighthearted.

TECHNIQUES:
HOW TO TEST A STORY WITHOUT BREAKING A SWEAT

1. ASK INNOCENT, POINTED FOLLOW-UPS

Bullshitters dread follow-up questions because their stories aren't built to withstand scrutiny. The trick? Frame your questions as curious and non-threatening while exposing the weak spots.

Example:

Your friend brags, "I once dated a backup dancer for Beyoncé."

Instead of rolling your eyes, ask, "That's so cool! Which tour did they work on?" Watch their confidence shift to hesitation. They'll either double down with more nonsense or pivot so fast that they leave a breeze behind.

Pro Tip: The key is to stay casual. Politeness disarms them, making it harder for them to dodge the details.

2. CROSS-CHECK DETAILS

Bullshitters often forget their own lies, creating contradictions over time. Keep a mental note of their claims; you'll eventually catch them tangled in their web.

Example:

Last week, your coworker declared, "I hate dogs." Today, they're dog-sitting for a celebrity friend. Casually mention, "I thought you didn't like dogs?" and watch them scramble to reconcile their conflicting narratives.

Pro Tip: Approach this with curiosity, not accusation. A simple observation is enough to make them falter.

3. PLAY DUMB AND LET THEM TALK

Pretending to be impressed encourages the bullshitter to elaborate, often leading to hilariously exaggerated details that reveal the truth.

Example:

Your friend claims they "partied with Mick Jagger in Ibiza." Instead of skepticism, say, "That's amazing! What's he like in person?" When they respond with something generic like, "Oh, super chill," follow up with, "What's his drink of choice? I bet it's something unique." The more they improvise, the more absurd their story becomes.

Why It Works: Genuine stories have vivid, consistent details. Bullshit collapses under pressure.

HILARIOUS SCENARIOS: SPOTTING BS IN THE WILD

SCENARIO 1: THE ROCK STAR CONNECTION

Friend: "I totally know Harry Styles. We hung out after one of his concerts."

You: "Wow, that's awesome! What's his favorite song to perform live?"

Friend: Long pause. "Oh, he didn't say, but he's super chill."

You: "What was the venue like?"

Friend: longer pause "Uh, it was this small, intimate place... you wouldn't have heard of it."

Translation: They've never met Harry Styles or been to his concert.

SCENARIO 2: THE SOCIAL MEDIA INFLUENCER

Coworker: "I'm working on becoming an influencer. My TikTok is blowing up right now."

You: "That's so cool! What's your handle? I'd love to follow you."

Coworker: "Oh, it's not public yet. But trust me, it's huge."

You: "How many followers do you have?"

Coworker: nervous laugh. "It's not about numbers, you know?"

Translation: Their "blowing up" account has three followers, including their mom.

SCENARIO 3: THE FITNESS ENTHUSIAST

Friend: "Honestly, I've been so into fitness lately. I work out every day."

You: "That's awesome! What's your favorite exercise?"

Friend: "Oh, you know… general stuff. Cardio. Weights."

You: "Cool! What's your go-to playlist?"

Friend: "Uh, I just listen to whatever's on."

Translation: Their "workout routine" involves scrolling Instagram in athleisure wear.

WHY THESE TECHNIQUES WORK

These strategies work because they're non-confrontational. You're not accusing anyone of lying outright; you're simply asking questions, staying curious, and letting them reveal the truth themselves. Bullshitters thrive on vague claims and your willingness to let things slide. By gently challenging their stories, you take away their safety net.

The best part? They often dig their own holes without realizing it, giving you the satisfaction of exposing the nonsense with minimal effort.

Practical Takeaways: Build Your BS Radar

- **Ask Questions:** Specific questions force bullshitters to think on their feet, where they often stumble.
- **Be Observant:** Pay attention to inconsistencies. Contradictions are the quickest way to spot a lie.
- **Stay Calm:** Avoid being confrontational and let their stories collapse under their own weight.

INTERACTIVE EXERCISE: SPOT THE BS

Put your skills to the test. Can you identify the BS in these statements?

"I once dated a Victoria's Secret model, but she doesn't like being talked about."

"My uncle invented Velcro, but he doesn't get credit for it."

"I'm fluent in French but don't like speaking it in public."

Answers:

BS. (If it's true, why bring it up?)

BS. (Velcro's invention is well-documented. Nice try.)

BS. (Fluency doesn't hide, it's just missing.)

Bullshitters might think they're masters of disguise, but with your newly honed BS radar, you'll see through their tales faster than a toddler sees through a game of peek-a-boo. The next time someone drops a dubious claim, smile, ask a question or two, and let their story trip over its own shoelaces. After all, watching them unravel is the real entertainment. Just grab the popcorn.

Everyone has encountered moments when a story feels too good to be true, whether it's a friend claiming they "dated Victoria's Secret model" or a coworker insisting their TikTok is "blowing up." This chapter introduces essential techniques for spotting nonsense, equipping readers with the tools to test tall tales without confrontation. Effective strategies include asking innocent yet pointed follow-ups, cross-checking details for inconsistencies, and playing dumb to encourage overelaboration. These non-confrontational approaches help expose BS by letting the storyteller trip over their own fabricated details, often in amusingly apparent ways.

The magic of these techniques lies in their subtlety. By staying curious and calm, you challenge claims without outright accusations, creating a low-pressure environment where contradictions and exaggerations reveal themselves naturally. Whether spotting contradictions in a fitness enthusiast's routine or questioning an influencer's "exploding" TikTok account, these methods allow you to see through BS while keeping the interaction lighthearted. The key takeaway? Let bullshitters dig their own holes. It's both effective and entertaining.

CHAPTER 7

WHEN TO CALL IT OUT

Spotting bullshit is one thing; deciding what to do about it is another. It's like being at a karaoke bar when someone's butchering Bohemian Rhapsody. Do you laugh it off and let them finish, or hit the stop button to spare everyone else? Not every tall tale or blatant lie needs to be tackled, and that's where judgment comes in.

This chapter is your guide to handling BS with finesse, whether to strike, let it slide, or respond with just the right amount of wit. With these tools, you'll navigate the minefield of nonsense without unnecessary drama.

TO STRIKE OR LET IT SLIDE?

Not all BS warrants your time or energy. Here's how to categorize it:

CATEGORY 1: HARMLESS BS

This type of BS is like too much frosting on a cupcake: unnecessary but mostly harmless. Examples include a coworker bragging about their karaoke skills or your aunt flaunting her "authentic" designer handbag that says Prada. It's often born from insecurity or a need for attention.

What to Do: Smile, nod, and move on. Bursting their bubble doesn't add value; it makes you look petty.

Inner Monologue: Sure, Jan. You crushed "Sweet Caroline." I'm sure Neil Diamond is reconsidering his career.

CATEGORY 2: HARMFUL BS

This is where BS gets serious claims that can damage reputations, sabotage careers, or hurt others. Think of a coworker taking credit for your ideas in a meeting or someone spreading hurtful rumors for attention.

How to Respond: Calmly address the lie with facts. Stay professional and focused on the issue, not the person.

Example:

Coworker: "The marketing strategy was entirely my idea."

You: "I remember presenting that concept during our last brainstorming session. I think we both contributed, don't you?"

Outcome: The truth is clarified without creating unnecessary conflict.

CATEGORY 3: OUTRAGEOUS BS

Outrageous BS is the kind that practically begs for attention. Think of your cousin claiming they were "this close" to starring in The Fast and the Furious or your friend insisting they "once gave Beyoncé directions to a gas station."

How to Respond: When the BS is absurd, lean into the humor. A witty or sarcastic response can deflate their claim without escalating the situation.

THE ART OF THE SARCASTIC COMEBACK

Sarcasm is a powerful tool for handling outrageous BS. It lets you call out nonsense without turning the conversation confrontational. Here are some go-to comebacks:

1. "Oh, were you there when Napoleon crossed the Alps, too?"

For anyone spouting grandiose historical or overly dramatic stories.

Example:

Them: "Napoleon's strategy during the Alps crossing was flawed."

You: "Oh, were you there? Did he take your advice?"

2. "You should write a memoir. Call it Stuff That Never Happened."

Perfect for those whose lives seem like a Netflix series, only fictional.

Example:

Them: "I was scouted for the Olympics, but I tore my ACL right before tryouts."

You: "Wow. That memoir's going to be a bestseller fiction, obviously."

3. "Let me call Guinness the Biggest Lie of the Year."

Best reserved for claims so outrageous they belong on a reality TV show.

Example:

Them: "I outran a bear while hiking in Alaska."

You: "Amazing. I'll call Guinness, and they'll want to document this."

WHEN SARCASM ISN'T THE ANSWER?

Not every situation calls for wit. When professionalism or tact is required, stick to the facts and avoid humor that might escalate tension.

Example:

Them: "I'm the one who closed that big client deal."

You: "Actually, that was a collaborative effort. Let's make sure the team gets credit."

Why It Works: It's polite and professional and shuts down false claims without room for debate.

REFLECTION QUESTIONS: SHOULD YOU CALL IT OUT?

Before you decide to confront BS, consider these questions:

Is it worth it? Will addressing this make a difference, or is it just harmless fluff?

Will it help or hurt the situation? Sometimes, letting them stew in their own nonsense is more effective.

Are you ready for the fallout? Even harmless corrections can ruffle feathers, so choose your battles wisely.

PRACTICAL TAKEAWAYS: HOW TO HANDLE BS

Choose Your Battles: Save your energy for harmful or outrageous lies that have real consequences.

Stay Cool: Whether you're being sarcastic or straightforward, keep your tone light and composed.

Have Fun: Enjoy the humor in calling out BS when the stakes are low.

INTERACTIVE EXERCISE: STRIKE OR SLIDE?

Let's test your BS radar. Decide whether to call it out or let it slide:

Your coworker claims they're "best friends" with the CEO.

Your friend takes credit for a joke you made in a group chat.

Your cousin swears they "hacked into a government system to stop a cyberattack."

Answers:

Let it slide unless they're using the claim for personal gain.

Politely call it out: "Glad you liked my joke enough to repeat it!"

Strike with humor: "Wow, when's the Netflix documentary airing?"

PRACTICAL TAKEAWAY

Confronting bullshit is like playing verbal Jenga: you can poke at the nonsense just enough to topple the tower, or you can let it wobble amusingly while you grab another drink. Whether you call it out, let it slide, or throw in a zinger for good measure, remember: handling BS isn't just about the truth; it's about ensuring the interaction is as entertaining as the story.

Navigating bullshit isn't just about spotting it. It's about knowing when and how to respond. This chapter equips you with strategies to handle nonsense effectively, from deciding when to confront it to using humor or facts to diffuse the situation. Bullshit can be harmless fluff, harmful manipulation, or outright absurdity, and your approach should depend on the type. Harmless BS, like exaggerated karaoke skills or a "designer" handbag, often doesn't need a response—smile, nod, and move on. Harmful BS, like a coworker taking credit for your ideas, requires calm professionalism and fact-based corrections. Outrageous BS—like tales of stopping cyberattacks or hanging out with celebrities can often be addressed with playful sarcasm.

When calling out BS, the goal isn't to humiliate but to navigate the situation with tact and, when appropriate, humor. Sarcastic comebacks, like "Hold on, let me call Guinness," work wonders for outrageous claims, while polite corrections suit professional scenarios. However, not every instance of BS is worth the effort. Consider the stakes: is it worth the potential fallout or just harmless exaggeration? Knowing when to strike, let it slide, or play along is the key to handling nonsense with finesse. Remember, managing BS isn't just about truth. It balances honesty, humor, and grace for the best outcome.

CHAPTER 8

OUT-BULLSHITTING A BULLSHITTER

Sometimes, the best way to deal with bullshit isn't by exposing it; it's by outdoing it. Why call someone out when you can up the ante, raise the absurdity, and leave them scrambling in a sea of their own nonsense? Welcome to the art of out-bullshitting a bullshitter.

Think of it as verbal judo: rather than resisting their tall tales, you use their momentum to your advantage. They say they "met Elon Musk at a house party"? Wonderful you were his keynote speaker. They're training for a triathlon? Impressive, you just ran a marathon backward to raise awareness for kangaroo conservation. With a straight face and unwavering confidence, your counter-BS will steal the show.

TECHNIQUES: HOW TO OUT-BS LIKE A PRO

Mastering the art of out-bullshitting requires three key techniques: confidence, **escalation, and timing.**

1. MATCH THEIR CONFIDENCE

Bullshit thrives on confidence. The more self-assured someone sounds, the more believable they seem. Your job? Match their energy no matter how ridiculous your claim, and deliver it with unwavering conviction.

Example:

Them: "I hiked Mount Everest with just a water bottle and granola bars."

You: "That's impressive. I did it barefoot because I wanted to 'connect with nature.' The Sherpas gave me an honorary title."

You take control of the conversation by matching their confidence and outshining their claim. Bonus points for the straight fac

2. USE THE "YES, AND..." TECHNIQUE

Borrowed from improv comedy, the "Yes, and…" technique allows you to agree with their claim while one-upping it. This keeps the tone playful and forces them to double down or retreat.

Example:

Them: "I wrestled a shark while snorkeling in Australia."

You: "Yes, and I wrestled a dolphin. It wasn't attacking me; I just wanted to see if I could win. We're friends now."

By taking their story further, you highlight its absurdity without outright dismissal.

3. ESCALATE THE ABSURDITY

Out-bullshitting isn't about subtlety; it's about going big. The more outrageous your counterclaim, the harder it is for them to keep up.

Example:

Them: "I got scouted by a modeling agency at the airport."

You: "Oh, I know the feeling. I got scouted by three agencies while stuck in traffic. They sent drones to deliver the contracts. Apparently, my profile looked incredible through the windshield."

Escalating the absurdity guarantees you steal the spotlight while leaving them floundering.

THE BULLSHIT OLYMPICS: VERBAL DUELS IN ACTION

Scenario 1: Shark Wrestler vs. Octopus Whisperer

Friend: "I wrestled a shark while diving in Hawaii. It was intense, but I escaped."

You: "That's incredible. I befriended an octopus in Bali. We played chess for an hour, which obviously allowed me to win."

Adding an unexpected twist ensures their story becomes the second most interesting in the room.

Scenario 2: Celebrity Encounter Escalation

Friend: "I met Taylor Swift once. She said she loved my scarf."

You: "No way! I met her at a farmer's market. She asked me for advice on picking the best avocados. I taught her my secret technique."

The humor keeps the tone playful while subtly undercutting their claim.

Scenario 3: The Overachiever One-Up

Coworker: "I just got back from a silent meditation retreat. It was life changing."

You: "Wow, I went to a reverse silent retreat where everyone talks nonstop. It was equally life-changing but for completely different reasons."

This response keeps the interaction light while making it impossible for them to one-up you.

WHY OUT-BS WORKS

Bullshitters thrive on being the most interesting person in the room. Out-bullshitting them flips the script, forcing them to keep up with your absurdity. The beauty of this approach is its playfulness: you're not aggressively calling them out; you're joining their game and taking it to the next level.

You reclaim control of the conversation by outdoing them and injecting humor into the exchange. Even better, you leave your dignity intact and maybe a few laughs.

PRACTICAL TAKEAWAYS: MASTERING THE CRAFT

Stay Confident: No matter how ridiculous your counter-BS, deliver it with conviction.

Keep It Playful: The goal is to entertain, not humiliate.

Read the Room: Know your audience. Some people appreciate humor, while others might take themselves too seriously.

INTERACTIVE EXERCISE: OUT-BS PRACTICE

Try crafting your own responses to these common BS scenarios:

Friend: "I once flew first-class for free because the airline upgraded me on the spot."

Coworker: "I've been to every continent except Antarctica."

Cousin: "I can eat 50 hot dogs in one sitting."

Suggested Responses:

"That's amazing! I once flew in the cockpit because the pilot wanted my advice on turbulence."

"Antarctica's incredible! I stayed in an Airbnb igloo. It came with free penguin sled rides."

"Fifty? That's impressive. I once entered a hot dog-eating contest but got disqualified for eating too fast. They said it wasn't fair to the others."

Out-bullshitting a bullshitter is the conversational equivalent of jazz: it's about improvising, escalating, and enjoying the absurdity without ever missing a beat. So, the next time someone tells you they've got the secret to unlocking the human genome because they Googled it once, smile, lean in, and let them know you've already submitted your Nobel Prize-winning work on decoding dolphin language. Remember, the goal isn't to win; it's to laugh so hard that you both forget who started the nonsense in the first place.

Sometimes, the best way to handle bullshit is to outshine it with your own absurdity. You can turn tall tales into a playful competition by matching confidence, escalating the story, and adding humor. The art of out-bullshitting relies on verbal judo using their energy to fuel your counterclaim. When someone brags about wrestling sharks or meeting celebrities, lean in with tales of befriending octopuses or advising Taylor Swift on avocados. The more ridiculous your response, the harder it becomes for the original storyteller to keep up, shifting the spotlight back to you.

This technique works because bullshitters thrive on being the center of attention. Outdoing their nonsense disrupts that dynamic, turning the interaction into a game where everyone gets to laugh. However, the key is to stay playful and read the room. This approach works best with confidence and humor, ensuring the interaction entertains rather than embarrasses. Next time someone boasts about improbable feats, channel your inner storyteller, craft an even wilder narrative, and enjoy the hilarious chaos that follows. After all, if you can't beat the bullshit, you might as well out-BS it.

CHAPTER 9

LEVELS OF MASTERY

Welcome to the Bullshit Olympics, where everyone competes, but only a select few claim golds. Whether dodging, detecting, or delivering it, BS is a universal skill. The question isn't whether you are part of the game but how skilled you are.

This chapter serves as your roadmap to mastery, guiding you from a novice fumbling through fibs to an expert navigating nonsense with finesse. Ready to level up? Let's see where you stand.

LEVEL 1: BEGINNER – DODGING YOUR OWN PITFALLS

At the beginner level, you're like a baby deer on shaky legs, blissfully unaware of the holes in your stories. Your intentions are good. You want to impress, entertain, or avoid conflict, but your execution needs serious work.

Common Mistakes:

Forgetting Your Own Lies: One day, you're an avid hiker; the next, you can't name a single trail.

Overcomplicating Stories: A simple anecdote about a bad date spirals into an implausible saga of cults and car chases.

Doubling Down: Instead of admitting you stretched the truth, you pile on more nonsense, turning a small fib into a full-blown soap opera.

How to Improve:

Stick closer to the truth. A little flair is fine, but keep it believable.

Know when to stop. Not every story needs to sound like a movie trailer.

Practice consistency. If you're embellishing, remember your details.

Pro Tip: Confidence might get you started, but credibility will keep people listening. Focus on balancing both.

LEVEL 2: INTERMEDIATE – SPOTTING BS EFFORTLESSLY

At this stage, you've graduated from spinning unfiltered BS to spotting it with precision. Phrases like "Trust me" or "Honestly, I wouldn't lie" trigger your internal alarm faster than a phishing email promising you a free yacht.

Your superpower is pattern recognition, which is noticing inconsistencies and contradictions. Last week, Karen was "deathly allergic to cats." This week, she's a proud volunteer at a cat sanctuary? Your radar doesn't miss a beat.

The Challenge

Calling out every fib is tempting, but not all battles are worth fighting. Pointing out someone's bogus marathon claim might be satisfying at the moment, but is it worth the awkward silence that follows? Probably not.

Pro Tips for Refinement:

- Use subtle prompts. "Really? That's fascinating. Tell me more" often unravels a story without confrontation.
- Let harmless nonsense slide unless it affects you or others. Watching someone squirm in their own web of lies is far more entertaining.

Save your energy for harmful or outrageous claims.

LEVEL 3: EXPERT – OUTSMARTING MANIPULATORS WITH STYLE

Welcome to the top tier. As an expert, you don't just spot BS but dismantle it precisely. You've mastered the art of calling out nonsense without hostility, leaving the bullshitter tangled in their own web.

Your Superpowers:

- **The Gentle Call-Out:** A subtle "That's interesting. How exactly did that work?" often prompts a flurry of backtracking.
- **Strategic BS Deployment:** You use humor or harmless fibs to entertain, diffuse tension, or smooth over awkward moments.
- **Knowing When to Walk Away:** Some lies aren't worth your time. Let the bullshitter stew while you enjoy the show.

Advanced Techniques:

- **The Reverse Uno:** Flip their claim with a probing question.

Example:

Them: "I know a top Hollywood producer."

You: "That's amazing! Which studio do they work with?"

- **The Compliment Trap:** Disarm them with flattery, then watch them stumble.

Example:

Them: "I'm training for an ultra-marathon."

You: "Incredible! What's your favorite workout? Any tips?"

- **Walking Away:** Not every lie deserves your energy. Sometimes, the best move is to let them dig their own grave.

REFLECTION QUESTIONS: WHAT'S YOUR LEVEL? ASK YOURSELF

Do you often catch yourself embellishing stories?

Can you spot a tall tale the moment it starts?

Have you ever diffused a manipulative situation with charm and wit?

If you answered "yes" to most, congratulations, you're leveling up!

PRACTICAL TAKEAWAYS: YOUR PATH TO MASTERY

Beginner: Focus on self-awareness and keeping your stories consistent.

Intermediate: Sharpen your BS radar and pick your battles wisely.

Expert: Use wit and timing to navigate nonsense gracefully while maintaining integrity.

INTERACTIVE EXERCISE: WHAT'S YOUR LEVEL?

Here are some common BS scenarios. How would you respond?

Coworker claims they're "best friends" with a famous influencer.

A friend insists they've traveled to 40 countries but can't name more than three.

Cousin swears they once dated a pop star.

Suggested Responses:

Beginner: Smile and nod. Move on.

Intermediate: "Wow, which country was your favorite? Why?"

Expert: "That's incredible! Did they write a song about you?"

Mastering the art of bullshit is like becoming a ninja: you don't fight every battle, but when you do, it's swift, precise, and leaves everyone in awe. Whether you're dodging pitfalls, artfully exposing nonsense, or gracefully flipping claims back onto their originators, remember: it's not about winning the game; it's about playing it with style. Because in the end, a true master doesn't just survive the bullshit they thrive in it, one clever comeback at a time.

Bullshit is everywhere, but navigating it requires skill and finesse. This chapter outlines three levels of mastery in dealing with nonsense: Beginner, Intermediate, and Expert.

At the beginner level, you may struggle with embellishments, forgetting your lies, or overcomplicating stories. To improve, focus on consistency, stick closer to the truth, and learn when to stop adding unnecessary flair. Confidence and credibility should work hand-in-hand at this stage.

As an Intermediate, your BS radar becomes sharp. You can easily spot inconsistencies and subtle red flags, like contradictory claims or suspiciously vague stories. However, the challenge lies in knowing which nonsense to address and which to ignore. Harmless fluff isn't worth the effort, while harmful or outrageous lies may warrant subtle, non-confrontational prompts that unravel the story.

The Expert level is where mastery shines. Here, you detect BS and outmaneuver it with precision and style. You can call out manipulators without hostility using humor, wit, and strategic questions, leaving them to stumble in their web of lies. Advanced techniques, like flipping claims back on their originators or gracefully walking away, demonstrate confidence and control. Whether you're dodging pitfalls, exposing nonsense, or diffusing awkward moments, a true master thrives in the game with elegance and charm.

CHAPTER 10

WHY DO PEOPLE BULLSHIT?

Let's cut to the chase: everyone bullshits. Yes, even you. Why? Because the unvarnished truth is often messy, mundane, or, frankly, underwhelming. Bullshit, on the other hand, adds spice to life. It makes you sound smarter, cooler, or more interesting than you might actually be. But what fuels this universal habit? What drives us to stretch the truth or sprinkle extra drama onto the everyday?

In this chapter, we explore the three main reasons people bullshit: ego, fear, and boredom. Whether it's claiming you "met Beyoncé at Target" or padding your resume with "Excel wizard," there's always a deeper motivation behind the exaggeration.

EGO: LOOK AT ME, I'M AWESOME

Ah, the ego. That persistent little voice whispering, "You need to seem more impressive." Ego-fueled bullshit isn't just about impressing others. It's about crafting a version of yourself you wish were true. It's less about who you are and more about who you want people to think you are.

Consider the times you've conveniently left out less flattering details, like the part where your "epic hike" involved getting lost for two hours.

Or when you exaggerated your role in a team project to make it sound like you carried the whole team. Ego-driven BS inflates your achievements to earn a fleeting moment of admiration.

Social media is the perfect playground for this. Nobody shares the photo of their soggy leftovers with the caption, "Barely surviving." Instead, it's avocado toast paired with "Living my best life!" You might've cried in your car before eating that toast, but it's all about the highlight reel online.

FEAR: PLEASE DON'T JUDGE ME

Fear-based bullshit isn't about showing off, it's about self-preservation. It sneaks in when the stakes are high and you're desperate to avoid judgment, embarrassment, or consequences.

Picture this: Your boss asks if you've started that report, and you confidently reply, "Almost done!" (Translation: you haven't started.) Or when someone mentions The Godfather, you nod along, terrified to admit you've never seen it. Fear-driven BS is about dodging the awkwardness of admitting a shortfall, whether it's your lack of preparation or ignorance about a cultural touchstone.

This type of BS often makes guest appearances on first dates, job interviews, and family reunions. Maybe you tell your date you "love cooking" even though your idea of a gourmet meal is microwaved mac and cheese. Or you insist you're "super close" with your cousin, even though your last conversation was on Facebook three years ago. Fear-based BS isn't about dazzling; it's about surviving.

BOREDOM: LET'S MAKE LIFE INTERESTING

Sometimes, BS isn't about ego or fear; it's simply about making life less dull. The truth? You spent the weekend binge-watching Dateline. The BS version? You "ended up at an underground jazz club," where a stranger bought you drinks because you "totally resemble Bob Dylan."

Boredom-fueled BS often showcases creativity. Remember that kid in school who swore their uncle was an astronaut? Or the friend who claimed they "hung out with Drake" but couldn't name a single song? These stories aren't malicious; they're attempts to add excitement to an otherwise routine day.

Let's face it: nobody wants to hear about how you organized your sock drawer. So, instead, you embellish. Suddenly, your coworkers hear about the "crazy bar crawl," and you go on, omitting the part where the wildest thing you drank was chamomile tea.

THE BULLSHIT TRIFECTA: WHEN MOTIVATIONS COLLIDE

Here's the kicker: most bullshit doesn't fall neatly into one category. Often, it's a cocktail of ego, fear, and boredom working together to create the perfect storm of nonsense.

Imagine you're at a party, and someone asks what you've been up to. Instead of saying, "Not much," you claim you're working on a "side hustle." Ego drives you to appear ambitious. Fear stops you from admitting you spent the weekend reaching 90 Day Fiancé. Boredom pushes you to embellish details about your "thriving Etsy shop."

The result? A web of half-truths that might impress the room until someone starts asking for specifics.

REFLECTION QUESTIONS: WHY DO YOU BS?

Take a moment to reflect:

Have you ever exaggerated a story to make it sound cooler?

Do you say "yes" to avoid looking clueless, even when you have no idea what's going on?

What's the wildest BS you've told purely out of boredom?

Understanding your motivations is the first step toward managing your BS and maybe even cutting back when it's unnecessary.

'Bullshit isn't just a habit; it's an art form born from the messy, insecure, and endlessly creative corners of the human mind. Whether inflating our egos, dodging the harsh spotlight of judgment, or spicing up a mundane story, BS is as universal as bad dance moves at a wedding. So, the next time you feel the urge to claim you've trained with Shaolin monks or dined with Beyoncé, pause and ask: Am I trying to impress, escape, or have some fun? And remember, a little bullshit makes life interesting, but too much can leave you tangled in your own tall tales.

Everyone engages in bullshit, whether to impress, protect themselves, or add excitement to the mundane. At its core, BS serves as a creative escape from the unvarnished truth, which often feels too ordinary. Ego-driven BS stems from a desire to appear more accomplished or impressive through inflating achievements or curating flawless social media personas. It's not about who you are but who you want others to see. On the flip side, fear-based BS is self-preservation in disguise. It shows up when people want to avoid judgment or embarrassment, such as fabricating progress on a project or pretending to be familiar with cultural references to fit in.

Lastly, boredom-fueled BS exists purely to spice up life. It turns a dull weekend into an embellished adventure or creates fantastical stories for fun. These lies are less about manipulation and more about entertainment. Most BS is a cocktail of ego, fear, and boredom working in tandem, creating stories that serve multiple purposes: to impress, dodge scrutiny, and keep conversations lively.

CHAPTER 11

THE PSYCHOLOGY OF BELIEVABILITY

Admit it: you've fallen for some outrageous bullshit before. Whether it was your coworker swearing they were "seconds away" from pitching a startup idea to Elon Musk or your friend recounting their heroic tracheotomy with a pen, you nodded along, captivated by the absurdity. But why? Why do some stories, no matter how implausible, bypass logic and land straight in your brain's "believable" category?

The answer lies in the psychology of believability. Bullshit works because it taps into a set of psychological triggers that make our brains go, "Maybe that is true." This chapter breaks down the sneaky tactics that make nonsense convincing, helping you spot it or spin it with finesse.

CONFIDENCE: THE POWER MOVE

Imagine someone at a party claiming they were once a backup dancer for Beyoncé. Your gut might scream, "No way!" but if they say it with unwavering confidence, steady voice, relaxed posture, and a casual sip of their drink, you might buy into it. Why? Because confidence is contagious. It's the golden ticket that makes even the wildest stories seem plausible.

Confident people don't hedge. They don't say, "I think I might have bumped into Taylor Swift once." They declare, "Taylor Swift complimented my scarf backstage." And because they radiate certainty, you hesitate to question them. After all, who wants to be the buzzkill in the room?

Pro Tip: Confidence doesn't equal truth. If someone's self-assured delivery feels too polished, it's time to dig deeper.

SPECIFICITY: DETAILS THAT DISTRACT

Want to make a story believable? Add some hyper-specific details. "I saw Tom Cruise once" is forgettable. But, "I saw Tom Cruise at a tiny café in Venice sipping a double-shot macchiato while reading a book on quantum physics" suddenly feels real. Why? Because our brains are wired to trust vivid imagery, even when it's fabricated.

Bullshitters know this and lean on details to sell their stories. The trick is to probe those details. Ask, "What was the café called?" or "What book was he reading?" Authentic details hold up; fake ones unravel faster than a bad alibi.

THE ECHO EFFECT

There's a reason marketers and politicians love repetition: it works. The Illusory Truth Effect, a psychological phenomenon where repeated statements start to feel true, means hearing the same claim repeatedly embeds it in your brain. Even if your logical side knows better, familiarity can override skepticism.

In everyday conversations, repetition works the same way. That coworker reminding everyone they "ran a half-marathon last year" isn't just sharing a fun fact. They're cementing a narrative. By the fifth mention, you'll recall their accomplishment like its gospel.

WHY WE FALL FOR IT

So, why do we fall for bullshit, even when it's clearly too good to be true? The answer comes down to two human traits: trust and effort avoidance.

Trust: Most of us operate on the assumption that people are honest. Treating every interaction like a cross-examination is exhausting, so we default to believing others even when they're stretching the truth.

Effort Avoidance: Fact-checking takes time and energy. Unless the claim has serious stakes, it's easier to nod along than whip out your phone to Google whether alpacas really spit fire.

HOW TO SPOT THE TRICKS

To sharpen your BS radar, look for these red flags:

- **Overconfidence:** If someone delivers their story with unshakable certainty, consider testing their claim. Genuine people often hedge with phrases like "I think" or "I believe."
- **Suspicious Specifics:** Hyper-detailed claims can either indicate authenticity or calculated deception. Follow up with probing questions to see how their story holds up.

- **Repetition Overload:** If you've heard the same point repeated multiple times, it's likely an attempt to cement credibility, not proof of truth.

PRACTICAL TAKEAWAYS

- **Test Their Confidence:** Ask open-ended questions to see if their certainty cracks under scrutiny.
- **Probe the Details:** Specifics should feel organic, not rehearsed. Challenge inconsistencies with curiosity, not confrontation.
- **Stay Wary of Repetition:** Familiarity isn't fact. If a claim keeps circling back, dig deeper before accepting it.

REFLECTION QUESTIONS

- When was the last time you believed a story because the person seemed so confident?
- Have you ever been fooled by a tale that felt genuine thanks to just enough detail?
- What's the most outrageous claim you've heard repeated until everyone accepted it as true?

The psychology of believability is like a magic trick: it dazzles, distracts, and leaves you momentarily convinced that the impossible is real. But once you know how it works, confidence, vivid details, and relentless repetition, you'll see through the act faster than a rabbit can disappear into a hat. So, the next time someone claims they've dined with Tom Cruise or wrestled a crocodile in Venice, smile knowingly and ask, "Which wine pairs best with a crocodile?" It's the perfect way to tell them you're not falling for the show.

Bullshit thrives because it taps into psychological triggers that make the implausible feel plausible. Confidence is key when someone tells a story with unwavering assurance; we instinctively trust their self-assurance, even if the tale feels far-fetched. The more certain they appear, the harder it is to question them without feeling like a buzzkill. Adding vivid, specific details is another powerful tool. A story with hyper-specific imagery, like "Tom Cruise sipping a macchiato in a Venetian café," tricks our brains into trusting it because we equate detailed descriptions with authenticity.

Repetition, known as the Illusory Truth Effect, also plays a significant role. The more we hear a claim, the more believable it feels, even if it's absurd. This explains why repeated assertions, whether a coworker bragging about a past accomplishment or a marketer selling a product, embed themselves in our minds as "truth." Human tendencies like trusting others and avoiding the effort of fact-checking further enable BS to slip through undetected.

To navigate these tricks, it's essential to recognize red flags: overconfidence, suspiciously specific details, and repeated claims that demand attention. Sharpening your BS radar involves testing confidence with open-ended questions, probing for inconsistencies in hyper-detailed stories, and remembering that familiarity doesn't equal fact. By understanding how believability works, you can enjoy the performance without falling for the illusion, turning absurd claims into opportunities for playful curiosity rather than unwitting acceptance.

CHAPTER 12

HOW SOCIETY REWARDS BULLSHIT

Let's not sugarcoat it. Bullshit isn't just tolerated; it's celebrated. From influencers selling us unattainable lifestyles to corporations drowning us in jargon, society often rewards confidence over competence. This chapter takes a closer look at how bullshit thrives, transforming mediocrity into stardom and empty promises into power. Welcome to a world where a slick delivery can trump substance, and a clever buzzword can land you the corner office.

THE INFLUENCER EFFECT: SELLING THE ILLUSION

Scroll through social media for ten minutes, and you'll encounter the influencer effect fully. These modern-day masters of embellishment have built careers on turning "fake it till you make it" into a business model. They sell you dreams: glowing skin, picture-perfect brunches, and stress-free mornings. The truth? Those effortless "candids" required staging, editing, and professional lighting hours.

Take the influencer hawking a $10 moisturizer they claim "changed their life." Do they even use it? Doubtful. But with a polished photo, a glowing caption, and a well-curated persona, they sell not the product but the fantasy. The message is clear: buy this, and your life could look like mine.

And it's not just about products. Influencers sell lifestyles that seem impossibly perfect. The "casual morning routine" shot, featuring golden sunlight and yoga poses, conveniently skips the part where they overslept, spilled coffee, and yelled at their dog for chewing their shoes. It's all about creating the illusion, and society laps it up.

CORPORATE CULTURE: WHERE BUZZWORDS REIGN SUPREME

If influencers are the apprentices of bullshit, corporate culture is the master class. The land of boardrooms and PowerPoints is fertile ground for meaningless jargon designed to impress without saying much of anything. Terms like "synergy," "disruption," and "scalable solutions" are thrown around with abandon, creating the illusion of innovation where there's none.

Consider the corporate mission statement. Have you ever read one and thought, wow, they're truly making the world a better place? Of course not. Most mission statements are vague platitudes meant to sound visionary while conveniently avoiding specifics.

And let's not forget job descriptions: "We need a self-starter who thrives in fast-paced environments." Translation? "Prepare to work long hours for mediocre pay." Then there's the PowerPoint presentation, a playground for corporate bullshit. A few slides filled with charts and jargon like "leveraging core competencies" can make the most mundane proposal seem revolutionary.

WHY BULLSHIT THRIVES

So why does society reward bullshit? Because it's easy to consume. Confidence and charisma often overshadow substance, making even the flimsiest claims appear credible. Whether an influencer selling a dream or a CEO pitching a buzzword-laden strategy, the performance often eclipses the truth.

Bullshit also feeds our desire for shortcuts. We want quick fixes and instant success. The influencer promises flawless skin with one product, and we want to believe it's that simple. The CEO assures us of "disruption," we assume they have a game-changing plan. The more polished the delivery, the more convincing the message.

Finally, there's FOMO, the fear of missing out. Suppose everyone else is raving about a new product or trend. In that case, it's tempting to jump on the bandwagon rather than risk being left behind.

THE COST OF REWARDING BULLSHIT

Here's the problem: celebrating bullshit has consequences. A charismatic leader can overshadow a competent one. A flashy marketing campaign can disguise a subpar product. When style takes precedence over substance, we lose sight of what matters.

But here's the good news: once you recognize the tactics that make bullshit thrive, you can navigate the nonsense with clarity. You don't have to buy into the detox teas, corporate jargon, or empty promises.

Instead, you can demand authenticity and celebrate those who prioritize substance.

HOW TO RESIST THE HYPE

Ask Questions: If it sounds too good to be true, dig deeper. What are they really saying?

Resist the Bandwagon: Just because everyone's raving doesn't mean it's worth your time or money.

Celebrate Authenticity: When you encounter someone who values substance, support them. They're rare in today's world.

REFLECTION QUESTIONS

- Have you ever regretted buying into an influencer's hype?
- What's the most meaningless corporate buzzword you've heard recently?
- How can you challenge the nonsense you encounter daily?

Society's love affair with bullshit is like a reality TV show; it's entertaining, flashy, and completely detached from reality. But now you know the game: influencers selling fantasies, corporations peddling buzzwords, and all of us, occasionally, buying into the hype. The next time someone pitches you a "disruptive, scalable solution" or a "life-changing moisturizer," smile, nod, and remember that the real win is seeing through the glitz and celebrating the rare gem of authenticity. Because while bullshit may steal the spotlight, substance is what truly stands the test of time.

Society doesn't just tolerate bullshit. It elevates it to an art form. With their curated lives and strategic product endorsements, influencers epitomize the art of selling illusions. Their "effortless" lifestyles, complete with perfectly staged photos and glowing captions, rarely reflect reality. From "life-changing" moisturizers to picture-perfect routines, the real product they sell is the fantasy of perfection. And yet, society buys in because these polished presentations tap into our desires for simplicity, quick fixes, and aspirational living.

In the corporate world, bullshit thrives through jargon, vague mission statements, and buzzword-heavy pitches that prioritize style over substance. Words like "synergy" and "disruption" create an aura of innovation, even when the reality is mundane. Job descriptions and PowerPoint presentations become playgrounds for ambiguity, masking mediocrity with overconfidence and meaningless flair. Society rewards these tactics because charisma often outshines competence, and we're drawn to the polished over the practical.

However, rewarding bullshit has its costs, from subpar leaders overshadowing capable ones to hype masking the value of authenticity. To resist, we must question what sounds too good to be true, resist bandwagon trends, and champion authenticity whenever we find it. While bullshit may dominate the spotlight, understanding its mechanics equips us to celebrate substance, a rare but timeless treasure amidst the noise.

CHAPTER 13

WHEN BS IS GOOD

THE NOBLE BULLSHITTER

By now, you've learned to spot, dodge, and dismantle bullshit with precision. But here's the twist: not all bullshit is bad. Sometimes, it's not only harmless but downright essential. It can save awkward conversations, smooth over social mishaps, and even inject a little humor into life's monotony.

Enter the Noble Bullshitter: the unsung hero of social dynamics. These are the people who wield bullshit responsibly, not to manipulate or deceive but to keep interactions flowing, prevent discomfort, and make moments more enjoyable. This chapter celebrates the art of harmless BS and equips you to use it ethically and effectively.

SOCIAL GLUE: BS THAT SAVES CONVERSATIONS

Picture this: you're at a family dinner, and your uncle starts recounting his "glory days" as a would-be professional boxer. Everyone knows it's exaggerated, but calling him out would lead to awkward silence or hurt feelings. Instead, you smile and say, "Wow, Uncle Joe, you must've been unstoppable!"

You've applied social glue to those harmless little fibs that keep conversations light and harmonious. Whether it's feigning interest in a coworker's niche hobby or complimenting a friend's slightly overcooked lasagna ("It's got such a unique flavor!"), these polite gestures help navigate tricky social waters.

The key to this type of BS is empathy. It's not about deceiving; it's about prioritizing kindness. Does your coworker really need to hear that their hobby bores you? Would your friend feel better knowing their lasagna missed the mark? Probably not. A touch of harmless embellishment keeps things pleasant without compromising your integrity.

WHEN BS SAVES THE DAY

Let's dive into a few moments when good-natured bullshit came to the rescue:

- **The Dreadful Dinner Date**

Halfway through your date, they reveal a passion for ceramic frog collections, and they're not stopping anytime soon. You're desperate to change the topic but don't want to offend. Enter harmless BS:

"Oh, that's interesting! I saw a documentary about how some Amazonian tribes use frog venom for hunting. Amazing stuff!"

True or not, you've successfully redirected the conversation and avoided a night of frog trivia.

- **Family Dinner Deflection**

Family gatherings are rife with nosy questions: "When are you getting married?" or "Why don't you visit more often?"

Instead of awkwardly fumbling, you respond with humor:

"I'm waiting for my royal wedding invite. Still holding out for Buckingham Palace!"

You've dodged the question, made them laugh, and kept the mood light.

- **The Small Talk Savior**

A coworker asks, "How was your weekend?" You could admit you binge-watched reality TV in your pajamas, but instead, you say:

"Great! Went on a hike. Fresh air, chirping birds, it was perfect!"

Did you actually hike? No. Does it matter? Also no. You've smoothed over a mundane moment with an effortless white lie.

THE ETHICS OF HARMLESS BS

You might wonder, "Isn't honesty the best policy?" Generally, yes. But honesty without tact can cause unnecessary discomfort. Harmless BS bridges the gap between raw truth and social harmony.

Here's how to keep your BS ethical:

- Don't Hurt Feelings: Your goal is kindness, not cruelty.
- Avoid Manipulation: Never use BS to coerce or mislead someone.
- Keep It Small: Stick to light, inconsequential fibs. No one needs a Shakespearean drama about your "career as a lion tamer."

Think of harmless BS as social seasoning, just enough to enhance the flavor of the moment but not so much that it overwhelms the dish.

INTERACTIVE PRACTICE: CRAFT YOUR NOBLE BS

Let's put your skills to the test. Here are a few tricky scenarios. Your mission? Come up with a harmless BS response to smooth over the moment.

The Awkward Haircut

Your coworker proudly shows off a haircut that... isn't their best look.

Possible BS Response:

"Wow, bold choice! It really shows off your confidence!"

The Oversharing Stranger

On a flight, the passenger next to you launches into a detailed story about their cat's dental surgery.

Possible BS Response:

"Wow, I had no idea cat dental care was so advanced. That's fascinating!"

The Burnt Dinner

A friend serves you a barely edible meal.

Possible BS Response:

"I love the texture! You really put your heart into this."

PRACTICAL TIPS FOR MASTERING HARMLESS BS

- Keep It Light: Aim for humor or politeness, not elaborate stories.
- Be Playful: A dash of humor makes harmless BS more effective and less awkward.

- Know When to Stop: Don't let a harmless fib spiral into an unnecessary saga.
- Read the Room: Adjust your approach based on how the other person responds.

REFLECTION QUESTIONS

- When did you last use harmless BS to smooth over a situation?
- Have you ever gone too far and had to backtrack? (It's okay; we've all been there.)
- What's your favorite go-to response for dodging tough or awkward questions?

Harmless BS is like social duct tape; it holds together the awkward, the boring, and the mildly uncomfortable moments of life without leaving behind a sticky mess. So, the next time you're cornered by frog trivia or confronted with a questionable haircut, remember: a little lighthearted embellishment isn't a crime; it's a kindness. After all, the Noble Bullshitter's motto is simple: keep it gentle, keep it funny, and always leave people smiling.

Not all bullshit is created equal. Some forms of BS, far from being harmful, play a vital role in social harmony, easing awkwardness and bringing humor to otherwise mundane moments. Enter the Noble Bullshitter, an empathetic master of harmless fibs who prioritizes kindness and connection over rigid honesty. Whether complimenting a questionable haircut or redirecting a dinner-table interrogation, this artful approach turns potentially uncomfortable interactions into moments of levity.

Harmless BS acts as social glue, smoothing over rough edges in conversations without crossing ethical boundaries. It shines in situations where honesty might cause unnecessary discomfort. For example, redirecting an overly passionate monologue about ceramic frog collections or deflecting nosy family questions with a humorous quip keeps things light without offending anyone. The key lies in small, inconsequential fibs prioritizing humor and tact rather than manipulation or deceit.

The Noble Bullshitter's skillset involves using harmless embellishments responsibly, ensuring they uplift rather than harm. Ethical guidelines like avoiding cruelty, keeping lies small, and steering clear of manipulation help keep the balance. You can navigate social dynamics with grace and charm by mastering playful responses and recognizing when BS can bring joy rather than harm. After all, the true mark of a Noble Bullshitter is leaving people smiling, even if the truth is slightly stretched along the way.

CHAPTER 14

THE ETHICAL BULLSHITTER'S GUIDE

So, you've learned how to spot, dodge, and wield BS. But now you're probably wondering, "Does this make me a bullshitter?" The answer is yes, but don't panic. The world doesn't need more liars; it needs ethical bullshitters. These people use BS responsibly, with humor and kindness, never crossing the line into manipulation or harm.

Think of this chapter as your Bullshit Code of Ethics, a practical guide to ensure your playful embellishments enhance social interactions rather than derail them.

RULE #1: NEVER BS ABOUT SERIOUS MATTERS

There's a difference between harmless exaggeration and crossing into dangerous territory. Ethical BS is reserved for lighthearted situations, not life-altering decisions.

- Claiming you "shook hands with Brad Pitt" to liven up a boring conversation? Harmless.

- Telling a coworker you love their amateur PowerPoint design? Kind and inconsequential.
- Lying about your qualifications during a job interview or giving false advice on an important issue? Harmful and unethical.

Relationships, health, and finances stick to honesty if the truth has real stakes. Ethical BS is meant to grease the wheels of conversation, not derail lives.

RULE #2: MAKE IT FUN, NOT HARMFUL

The best BS entertains, amuses, or smooths over social tension. It's not about making someone else feel small or manipulating them for personal gain.

THE FUN VS. HARMFUL TEST

- Saying, "I nailed a karaoke duet with Adele once"? Fun.
- Bragging about someone else's failure to boost your ego? Harmful.
- Exaggerating a snorkeling trip into a dolphin encounter? Playful and harmless.
- Pretending to be someone you're not to deceive? Not okay.

Ethical BS is a good joke; it makes people laugh without anyone feeling like the punchline. If your story adds a little sparkle without stepping on toes, you're doing it right.

RULE #3: KNOW WHEN TO STOP

Imagine You're at a party spinning a playful yarn about being mistaken for a celebrity. Everyone laughs. Then someone presses: "Who was it?"

Instead of bowing out gracefully, you double down: "Oh, Ryan Gosling, we could be twins!"

Now you're in a corner, fielding follow-up questions and spinning an increasingly absurd web to sustain your claim. Ethical BS has a shelf life. Once the laugh has landed, let it go. Doubling down turns harmless fun into cringe-worthy desperation.

Pro Tip:

When someone digs too deep, wink and say, "Okay, you got me!" A little self-awareness keeps the vibe light and your credibility intact.

THE ETHICAL BULLSHITTER'S CHECKLIST

Here's a quick guide to staying on the right side of harmless fun:

- Is it harmless? Will anyone feel hurt or betrayed by your BS? If not, you're good.
- Is it fun? Does it add humor or lighten the mood? If yes, carry on.
- Is it necessary? Sometimes, silence is better than a forced fib.
- Do you know when to stop? If your story feels like it's snowballing out of control, it's time to exit gracefully.

EXAMPLES OF ETHICAL BS IN ACTION

1. Saving Face at Work

Your boss asks for an update on a project you forgot to prepare for. Instead of panicking, you say:

"We're still refining ideas, but I'll have something concrete by tomorrow."

Translation: "I haven't started, but I will soon." No harm, no foul, and you've bought yourself time.

2. The Party Save

Someone corners you with an overly detailed story about their gluten-free dog food business. Instead of yawning, you reply:

"Oh, I read about that! It's fascinating how much the pet food market has evolved."

Did you actually read about it? Probably not. But you've kept the conversation polite without committing to a deep dive into hypoallergenic kibble.

3. Dodging Awkward Questions

Your family asks why you're not married yet. Instead of getting defensive, you quip:

"I'm still waiting for my royal wedding invitation. Buckingham Palace hasn't called yet."

You've deflected the nosy question with humor, keeping the conversation lighthearted.

INTERACTIVE EXERCISE: CRAFT YOUR ETHICAL BS

Try your hand at these scenarios:

- **The Party Save**

    Someone asks what you've been up to. Create a harmlessly embellished story to sound interesting.

- **The Awkward Compliment**

    A friend asks if you like your new hobby (interpretive dance). Craft a playful response that spares their feelings.

- **The Small Talk Escape**

    You're stuck in a boring conversation. What's your one-liner to gracefully pivot?

PRACTICAL TIPS FOR ETHICAL BS

- Keep It Light: Don't overcomplicate your fibs. Simple is best.
- Be Playful: A sense of humor makes harmless BS more palatable.
- Don't Overcommit: A little flair goes a long way; don't weave an elaborate backstory.
- Read the Room: If your audience looks skeptical, it's time to pivot or come clean.

REFLECTION QUESTIONS

- When did you last use harmless BS to smooth over an awkward situation?
- Have you ever taken BS too far and regretted it?
- What's your go-to ethical fib for dodging tough questions?

Ethical BS is like seasoning on a dish. It should enhance the moment, not overpower it. It smooths awkward situations, injects humor, and keeps social interactions afloat without sinking into deception. So, whether you're dodging nosy questions at a family dinner or crafting a playful save at a party, remember: a little well-placed BS, used responsibly, can make life's quirks all the more enjoyable. After all, the best bullshitters are the ones who leave people smiling.

Not all BS is harmful; using it responsibly can enrich social interactions, ease awkward situations, and bring humor to everyday life. Ethical bullshit involves playful embellishments that entertain or smooth over uncomfortable moments without crossing into deceit or manipulation. This chapter outlines the principles of ethical BS, emphasizing the importance of using it in lighthearted scenarios while steering clear of serious matters like health, finances, or relationships where honesty is crucial. Ethical BS thrives on kindness and humor. Whether complimenting a friend's burnt lasagna or deflecting nosy family questions with a witty quip, its purpose is to enhance interactions, not cause harm.

The guide to ethical BS encourages simplicity, self-awareness, and an understanding of when to stop. The best BS is light, inconsequential, and leaves people smiling, not skeptical. It's about adding levity and avoiding unnecessary drama while staying mindful of your audience and the situation. By keeping it fun, kind, and harmless, ethical BS becomes a valuable social tool that strengthens connections, diffuses tension, and ensures interactions remain enjoyable and positive. The Ethical Bullshitter prioritizes empathy and humor, leaving a lasting impression of charm and good-natured wit.

CHAPTER 15

LEAVING A LEGACY

BE A LOVABLE BULLSHITTER

You've made it this far; you're officially equipped to spot, counter, and even use BS when the situation calls for it. But what's the ultimate goal? It's not just about wielding nonsense with finesse; it's about being remembered as the lovable bullshitter, the one who could spin a yarn so captivating that nobody cared whether it was true.

The lovable bullshitter isn't manipulative or self-serving. They tell stories to connect, entertain, and inspire. They embellish not to deceive but to add a little flair to life's otherwise ordinary moments. If you leave behind a legacy, let it be one of humor, charm, and stories that unite people.

STORIES THAT ENTERTAIN NOT DECEIVE

The best bullshitters are storytellers, not liars. They turn mundane experiences into something worth retelling, adding just enough flair to keep people on to every word.

Example:

You went hiking, and the most interesting thing was a squirrel stealing your granola bar. Instead of saying, "A squirrel took my snack," you spin it like this:

"So, there I was, halfway up the mountain, when this squirrel appeared out of nowhere, eyes glinting with determination. He launched at me like a ninja, grabbed my granola bar, and disappeared into the woods without a sound. I swear, he looked back to smirk."

Is it exactly how it happened? No. But does it make people laugh and lean in for more? Absolutely. Great bullshit entertains while leaving just enough room for the listener to wonder if it might be true.

UNITE, DON'T DIVIDE

Good BS brings people together. It sparks shared laughter, curiosity, and connection. The key is to ensure your embellishments don't alienate or mock others.

Example of Connection vs. Division:

- **Divisive BS:** "My coworker actually believed I met Beyoncé. Can you believe how dumb they are?"
- **Lovable BS:** "I had my coworker convinced I was Beyoncé's tour manager for a week. I think they're still trying to figure it out!"

The first example isolates someone for a cheap laugh. The second invites everyone into the joke, making the story fun.

HOW BU CAN INSPIRE

BS isn't just about entertainment. It can also spark motivation or lift someone's spirits.

Imagine your friend is feeling discouraged about a career setback. You tell them a (slightly exaggerated) story about how you "totally nailed" a job interview while accidentally wearing mismatched shoes.

Does it matter if the shoe detail is real? Not at all. The point is that your story helps your friend laugh, see their situation differently, and maybe even feel a little braver about their own challenges.

BS doesn't have to be shallow. When used thoughtfully, it can inspire courage, creativity, or just a much-needed laugh.

CRAFTING A MEMORABLE BS LEGACY

A true BS legacy isn't built on deception, but on the moments you make brighter. People won't remember the exact details of your stories; they'll remember how you made them feel.

Tips for Crafting a BS Legacy:

- **Add Humor:** If your story doesn't make people laugh, it's not worth telling.
- **Keep It Light:** Avoid heavy or mean-spirited embellishments.
- **Poke Fun at Yourself:** Self-deprecating humor is charming and relatable.
- **Share the Spotlight:** Don't always make yourself the hero; let others shine in your stories.

INTERACTIVE SECTION: YOUR LEGACY STORY

Imagine it's 20 years from now, and someone is reminiscing about you as the lovable bullshitter. What story do you want them to tell?

PROMPTS TO GET YOU STARTED

- **The Great Adventure:** That time, you "helped" a lost tourist navigate the subway using a map you didn't understand.
- **The Office Hero:** You "saved the office" from disaster by fixing the coffee machine with a paperclip.
- **The Party Legend:** That unforgettable night when you "taught" a celebrity how to salsa (or so you claim).

Write your story, polish your delivery, and let it reflect the humor and charm you want to be remembered for.

LIVING IN A WORLD FULL OF NONSENSE

BS is everywhere, from social media to office small talk to family dinner table tall tales. But now, you're equipped to navigate it with grace, humor, and integrity.

Here's what you've mastered:

- **Spotting BS:** You can now sniff out nonsense a mile away. Whether it's a coworker bragging about "working smarter, not harder" or an influencer pretending their vacation wasn't completed, you know how to separate fact from fluff.
- **Navigating with Finesse:** You've learned when to call BS when to let it slide, and when to join in for the sake of a good laugh.

- **Using BS for Good:** You can spin harmless, entertaining, inspiring stories without crossing the line into deceit.

THE FINAL TAKEAWAY: BE THE BS PEOPLE LOVE

The world doesn't need more deception; it needs better stories. Be the person whose embellishments make life more interesting, whose nonsense brings people closer, and whose presence turns dull moments into unforgettable ones.

Next time someone catches your mid-story and asks, "Wait, is that true?" smile and reply:

"Does it really matter?"

Because, in the end, life is short, the truth is overrated, and a good story is priceless.

The ultimate goal of mastering BS isn't manipulation or deceit. It's to connect, entertain, and inspire through playful, harmless storytelling. The lovable bullshitter is someone who brings laughter and charm into social dynamics by spinning everyday moments into captivating tales that spark joy and curiosity. Whether embellishing a hiking story to make it hilarious or recounting a workplace mishap with creative flair, these embellishments unite rather than divide, fostering connection and shared laughter. A true BS artist understands that the magic lies in entertaining without alienating, keeping their stories light, self-deprecating, and inclusive.

A legacy of BS isn't about being remembered for outlandish lies but for the warmth, humor, and inspiration your stories bring to others. Ethical BS creates moments that lift spirits, motivate, and brighten someone's day. The lovable bullshitter's charm lies in their ability to make people feel good while leaving them wondering if the story might just be true. As you navigate a world full of nonsense, your legacy can be one of humor and connection, a reminder that a little harmless BS can make the journey far more enjoyable in a life often too serious.

CHAPTER 16

THE BS DETOX – CUTTING THE CRAP (TEMPORARILY)

TIME TO CLEAR THE AIR

Let's face it, you're swimming in bullshit. It's in your workplace meetings, social media feeds, family dinners, and even the little fibs you tell yourself. BS is everywhere, like glitter at a kid's birthday party: impossible to escape, no matter how hard you try.

But here's the kicker: some of it comes from you. Maybe you exaggerated the traffic when you were late for brunch. Or perhaps that "relaxing Sunday morning" photo took 30 minutes of pancake-stacking perfectionism. Don't worry, you're not alone. Everyone does it. But when the BS piles up too high, it's time to reset a BS Detox.

No need to panic. This isn't a forever thing. Think of it as a mental reset, like a juice cleanse for your brain only without the $14 smoothies.

WHY DETOX YOUR BS?

Bullshit sneaks up on you, turning little exaggerations into habits. Social media trains us to curate perfect lives, workplaces reward buzzwords over substance, and even casual conversations are laced with tiny lies. Before long, you stop noticing the nonsense, and worse, you start adding to it.

A week-long BS Detox helps you hit pause, recalibrate, and learn to recognize the fluff. By stepping away from the noise, you'll spot it faster, laugh harder, and think twice before contributing to it yourself.

RECOGNIZING YOUR BS TRIGGERS

Before cutting the crap, identify your biggest triggers. Here are some common culprits:

- **Social Media Curation**

Your "spontaneous" post of a perfect brunch wasn't so spontaneous. Social media thrives on exaggeration, and it's easy to fall into the trap of presenting an idealized version of yourself.

Trigger: Seeking validation or wanting to appear more impressive.

- **Workplace Survival Tactics**

Ever claimed you "love working under pressure" or "thrive in fast-paced environments"? Work culture often rewards inflated claims, pushing you to play along.

Trigger: Self-preservation or competitiveness.

- **First Dates and Small Talk**

When asked what you do for fun, you say "hiking" instead of admitting you binge-watch reality TV. You want to seem cooler, but spoiler: everyone does this.

Trigger: Fear of appearing boring or unremarkable.

- **Conflict Avoidance**

You tell a friend you're "just tired" when you're actually furious, or let your boss think you "missed the email" instead of admitting you ignored it.

Trigger: Discomfort with confrontation.

Understanding your triggers is half the battle. Once you know when and why you BS, you can consciously avoid falling into those patterns.

THE 7-DAY BS DETOX PLAN

Ready to detox? This step-by-step guide will help you temporarily ditch the fluff and embrace radical honesty.

DAY 1: RADICAL TRUTH

Your mission: Speak only the unembellished truth.

Example: Instead of saying you "waited forever" in line, say, "It took 10 minutes."

Tip: Pause before speaking and ask, "What's the real version of this story?"

DAY 2: HONEST SOCIAL MEDIA POST

Post something authentic no filters, no curated captions.

Example: "Worked out for 8 minutes today, then gave up and ate pancakes. No regrets."

Why It Works: People crave honesty. Watch how refreshing it feels.

DAY 3: ADMIT WHAT YOU DON'T KNOW

When you're stumped, say, "I don't know."

Example: "I don't know much about AI, but I'd love to learn."

Tip: Notice how free it feels to embrace not knowing instead of pretending.

DAY 4: POLITELY CALL OUT BS

Challenge little lies (nicely).

Example: When a coworker says, "I'm so swamped," ask, "What's been keeping you busy?"

Tip: Focus on curiosity, not confrontation.

DAY 5: OWN YOUR SELF-LIES

Identify one thing you've been Basing yourself on: your job, your fitness routine, or your "love" of kale smoothies. Write it down and acknowledge it honestly.

Goal: Free yourself from self-deception.

DAY 6: SAY NO WITHOUT EXCUSES

Stop overcommitting out of guilt.

Example: "Thanks for inviting me, but I will pass."

Why It Matters: Honesty builds respect and saves you time.

DAY 7: REFLECT AND RECHARGE

Take stock of the week:

- How often were you tempted to BS?
- What did you learn about yourself?
- What felt surprisingly good about being honest?

WHAT YOU'LL GAIN FROM THE DETOX

When you cut the fluff, surprising benefits emerge:

- Better Conversations: Authenticity fosters connection.
- Less Comparison: Letting go of curated perfection makes others' nonsense easier to ignore.
- More Energy: Being real is less exhausting than keeping up with your BS.
- Laughter: Radical honesty can be hilarious. Imagine saying, "I didn't finish the report because I got lost in otter videos."

POST-DETOX: RETURNING TO ETHICAL BS

The BS Detox isn't about becoming brutally honest forever; it's about recalibrating. Once you've reset, you can reintroduce ethical BS into your life with intention. Use it to add charm to your stories, not to manipulate or avoid responsibility.

Example:

Before Detox: "I crushed that presentation!"

After Detox: "It went well, but I was sweating bullets inside."

The BS Detox isn't about stripping life of its fun; it's about finding balance. By cutting through the noise and embracing a little raw honesty, you'll discover that reality, imperfections and all, is far more refreshing than a perfectly curated lie. So, detox, laugh at the absurdity of it all, and when you reintroduce bullshit, let it be the charming, harmless kind that brings people together, not the kind that makes life heavier. Because sometimes, the best nonsense is the one you know how to wield sparingly.

We live in a world overflowing with BS, from exaggerated social media posts to workplace jargon and even the small lies we tell ourselves. Chapter 16 introduces the concept of a BS Detox, a temporary reset designed to clear the mental clutter, recalibrate your nonsense radar, and embrace authenticity. This one-week cleanse isn't about abandoning all embellishment forever but about pausing to reflect on how BS influences our lives and relationships. By cutting through the fluff, you'll gain clarity, build more genuine connections, and rediscover the humor and simplicity of unfiltered honesty.

The 7-Day BS Detox Plan offers daily challenges, such as speaking only the unvarnished truth, posting authentically on social media, admitting what you don't know, and even politely calling out minor lies. Along the way, you'll uncover your BS triggers, from social media validation to fear of confrontation and learn to address them with mindfulness. Post-detox, you'll feel lighter, laugh more at the absurdity of life, and be ready to reintroduce ethical BS into your storytelling, using it as a tool for connection rather than avoidance or manipulation. Life, after all, is better with a balance of truth and a little harmless flair.

CHAPTER 17

BULLSHIT IN RELATIONSHIPS

Relationships, whether romantic or familial, are prime territory for bullshit to thrive. But not all BS is created equal. Some of it is harmless fun, making people laugh or creating lasting memories. However, there's a fine line between playful exaggeration and outright deceit. This chapter dives into two hotbeds of relationship VS dating and family interactions. It explores how to recognize it, when to call it out, and when to let it slide for connection.

THE DATING GAME: SWIPE RIGHT FOR STORIES

Modern dating is a playground for tiny lies and exaggerated truths. Everyone wants to put their best foot forward, often by polishing life's edges until they shine brighter than reality.

- "Adventurer" often means "went hiking once, took a selfie, and went home."
- "Fluent in Spanish" translates to knowing "queso" and "taco."
- "Entrepreneur" might just mean they have an Etsy shop with two sales.

These fibs are designed to impress but often unravel when you ask a follow-up question. Does someone claim they're an "avid reader"? Ask them what they're reading. They boast about summiting the Himalayas? Name a mountain and watch the panic set in.

HOW TO SPOT DATING BS

- Look for Consistency: If their stories don't align with their knowledge or behavior, you've found a red flag.
- Ask for Specifics: BS thrives in vagueness. A genuine person will welcome details; a bullshitter will flounder.
- Trust Your Gut: If something feels off, it probably is.

While small embellishments are forgivable, they're often born from a desire to connect bald-faced lies like claiming to be a "professional skydiver" without ever stepping onto a plane a deal breaker. Dating BS is tolerable in small doses but damaging if it undermines trust.

FAMILY BULLSHIT: WHERE LEGENDS ARE BORN

Family gatherings are the heart of harmless bullshit. The exaggerations here aren't about deceit but tradition, humor, and a shared sense of identity.

- Grandpa didn't just see a bear on his camping trip; he wrestled it.
- Dad didn't walk to school in mild weather; he braved blizzards uphill both ways.
- Uncle Joe was "one phone call away" from the NFL, or so he claims.

These tales aren't meant to fool anyone; they're stories that bring families together. They give a sense of legacy (however fictional) and provide much-needed comic relief during holiday dinners.

Why Family BS Works:

- It's Entertaining: A little drama keeps mundane stories alive across generations.
- It Bonds People: Everyone loves a good laugh at Dad's wildly exaggerated fishing story.
- It Teaches Lessons: While the facts might be shaky, the moral often holds true.

Family BS thrives because it's harmless. Nobody fact-checks Grandpa mid-monologue, and nobody wants to debunk Aunt Susan's "life-saving humanitarian trip" (which probably involved tipping a cab driver). It's not about accuracy; it's about creating moments that make gatherings memorable.

WHY BS FLOURISHES IN RELATIONSHIPS

So why do we bullshit the people closest to us? Because it's effective. BS can smooth over awkwardness, make us seem more impressive, and bring excitement to everyday interactions.

- On a date, saying you "love hiking" sounds better than admitting you only hike to the fridge for snacks.
- Grandpa's bear story overshadows the less impressive truth: he saw a squirrel and ran.
- Aunt Susan's humanitarian story inspires admiration even if the "starving kids" she helped were tourists looking for a snack bar.

The secret to successful BS lies in its believability. A small stretch of the truth can make a story charming. But go too far, like claiming to have "nearly joined NASA's Mars program," and you risk losing your audience.

TURNING BS INTO AN ART FORM

Not all BS is bad. Used sparingly and with charm, it can elevate conversations, diffuse tension, or turn a dull moment into something unforgettable. The trick is to keep it light and fun.

How to Master Lovable BS:

- Gauge the Room: Know your audience and tailor your nonsense to their vibe.
- Stay Self-Aware: Deliver your embellishments with a wink, letting people know you're in on the joke.
- Keep It Harmless: Your BS should entertain, not offend or deceive.

For example:

- On a date, saying, "I dabble in photography," is better than claiming you shot the cover of National Geographic.
- At a family dinner, embracing the story of Uncle Roy's pirate mop fight is more fun than correcting it.

Want to practice? At your next gathering, invent a harmless family legend. Perhaps Aunt Ida outran a bull in Pamplona, or Cousin Greg's chili recipe was stolen by a famous chef. The goal isn't to fool anyone; it's to create shared laughter and add a little sparkle to the moment.

WHEN TO CALL OUT BS

Sometimes, the bullshit gets out of hand. If a story veers into harmful territory, demeaning others, eroding trust, or pushing manipulative agendas, it's time to step in.

- **Be Gentle:** "That's a wild story! Are you sure about that?" can diffuse the tension without outright confrontation.
- **Pick Your Battles:** If the BS is harmless and entertaining, let it ride. But if it's crossing lines, speak up.
- **Stay Calm:** Calling someone out doesn't have to be confrontational. Focus on humor and curiosity instead of judgment.

PRACTICAL TAKEAWAYS

- **Spot the BS:** Learn to identify exaggerations versus outright lies.
- **Use BS Sparingly:** When you embellish, do it for fun, not manipulation.
- **Celebrate Family Legends:** They're part of what makes gatherings memorable.
- **Draw the Line:** Know when to let a story slide and when to call out harmful behavior.

Relationships and BS go together like peanut butter and jelly, sometimes a little sticky, but ultimately, they create something memorable. Whether you're spinning a harmless yarn on a first date or laughing along with Grandpa's wild tales of his youth, remember: it's all about intention. Use BS to bring smiles, not suspicion. After all, life's too short for dull stories and too long to tolerate harmful lies. Keep it fun and kind, and let a little sparkle elevate your connections.

Relationships, whether romantic or familial, are fertile ground for BS. In dating, small embellishments like claiming to "love hiking" or being an "entrepreneur" are common attempts to impress, though they often unravel under scrutiny. The dating world thrives on these polished truths, but trust is key, and bald-faced lies can damage budding relationships. Spotting dating BS involves looking for consistency, asking specific follow-ups, and trusting your gut.

Meanwhile, in family dynamics, BS often takes a more endearing form. Grandpa's bear-wrestling or Dad's uphill-in-the-snow school trek are classic family legends designed to entertain and bond rather than deceive. These exaggerated tales create shared laughter, foster connection, and often carry timeless lessons.

However, BS in relationships isn't always harmless. While it can smooth over awkwardness or add charm, crossing into harmful territory like eroding trust or demeaning others requires gentle intervention. The key to mastering relationship BS is intent: use it to elevate conversations, spark laughter, and create memorable moments, not to manipulate or offend. Whether you're laughing at Uncle Roy's pirate mop fight or spinning your playful yarns, BS can add sparkle to relationships when used sparingly and responsibly. After all, even with a pinch of embellishment, great stories make life more vibrant and relationships more meaningful.

CHAPTER 18

BULLSHIT IN THE WORKPLACE

There's one place where bullshit not only survives but thrives, it's the workplace. From jargon-filled meetings to performance reviews with vague praise, the professional world is practically engineered to churn out creative nonsense. Understanding this environment and navigating it is essential to survive and thrive. Let's explore how to spot, decode, and even use workplace BS effectively.

THE CORPORATE LANGUAGE OF NONSENSE

Corporate environments have perfected the art of sounding impressive without saying much. Words like synergy, scalability, and low-hanging fruit get tossed around like confetti at a New Year's party, yet their meaning is often elusive. For example:

- "Let's take this offline" = "I have no idea what to say right now, so let's pretend this is a longer discussion."
- "We're optimizing workflows" = "We've renamed an old process to sound innovative."
- "Pivoting strategies" = "We have no plan and are winging it."

Mastering this lingo is essential. Not because it adds value but because understanding it allows you to play along without feeling lost. When someone says, "We need to align on deliverables to achieve vertical optimization," a simple nod and reply like, "Absolutely, let's leverage cross-functional synergy," will keep you in the game.

MEETINGS: THE BS OLYMPICS

Meetings are the arena where workplace BS truly shines. Whether it's the overuse of buzzwords or endless monologues, they often achieve little while sounding important. To survive, you need tactics:

Deflect and Redirect:

- "Great point; let's revisit this after gathering more input." = "I'm stalling until I figure out what to say."
- "I'd love to hear others' thoughts first." = "Someone else take the fall, please."
- "That's worth exploring further." = "I have no idea what you're talking about."

Feign Engagement:

Master the "thoughtful nod" and "jotting down nonsense" techniques. Writing words like synergy or Q4 goals on a notepad gives the illusion of focus. Pair it with phrases like, "Interesting perspective. Can we dive deeper into that?" to appear invested.

Chart Theatre:

Impressive visuals can mask a lack of substance. Pie charts and colorful flow diagrams labeled with terms like performance alignment metrics may leave everyone nodding, even if the data means nothing. Pro tip: clap politely, but don't try deciphering it.

RECOGNIZING THE WORKPLACE BS AFICIONADOS

Workplace BS is an art, and some excel at it:

- **The Buzzword Machine:**

    They thrive on jargon, turning every task into a collaborative initiative and every problem into an opportunity for growth. Their sentences sound impressive but leave you scratching your head.

- **The Meeting Monopolize:**

    These are the people who speak to hear their own voices. They will overuse terms like KPIs and key takeaways while saying nothing actionable.

- **The Last-Minute Procrastinator:**

    This person crams work hours into the final stretch and brands it as thriving under pressure. Their procrastination magically transforms into a badge of honor.

- **The Chart Enthusiast:**

    They create visually stunning but meaningless presentations. Their graphs and slides are colorful and sleek, but their content is as empty as an overdue inbox.

WHY WORKPLACE BS PERSISTS

Corporate BS survives because it's easier to sound smart than to take meaningful action. Confidence in delivery often trumps substance. A statement like, "We're redefining strategic priorities," sounds forward-thinking. At the same time, a simple "Let's focus on what matters" risks being overlooked.

HOW TO NAVIGATE AND SUCCEED IN THE BS ZONE

While corporate BS can be frustrating, it doesn't mean you have to lose your authenticity. Here's how to stay ahead:

- **Learn the Language:**

  Use buzzwords sparingly to blend in, but don't rely on them entirely. Keep your contributions grounded to stand out when it matters.

- **Master the Redirect:**

  When caught off-guard, redirect attention with confidence. "I don't have the numbers now, but let's connect after the meeting" buys you time without appearing unprepared.

- **Appear Engaged:**

  Perfect your body language, nodding thoughtfully, jotting fake notes, and occasionally throwing out, "That's an important point to explore further," keeps you in the game.

- **Know When to Opt Out:**

  While BS can help you navigate tricky situations, don't let it define you. Genuine contributions build trust and credibility. Save the nonsense for when it's truly necessary.

PLAY THE GAME, DON'T BE THE GAME

The workplace may reward polished nonsense, but you don't have to become its champion. Recognize the BS, use it strategically, and focus on delivering value when it counts.

Next time someone says, "Let's leverage synergies to foster impactful solutions," smile, nod, and remind yourself you're playing the game, not falling for it. And that's how you win in a world powered by buzzwords and PowerPoint slides.

The workplace is a breeding ground for creative nonsense, where jargon-filled meetings and buzzword-heavy conversations dominate. Corporate lingo, such as "synergy" and "low-hanging fruit," often sounds impressive but lacks substance, leaving many wondering what was truly said. Meetings, referred to as the "BS Olympics," are arenas where these practices thrive, featuring tactics like vague buzzwords, overcomplicated visuals, and deflection strategies to mask a lack of actionable input.

Recognizing these patterns helps you navigate and decode the corporate language of nonsense. Common archetypes in this environment include the "Buzzword Machine," who thrives on jargon; the "Meeting Monopolize," who speaks without substance; and the "Chart Enthusiast," who dazzles with visuals that mean little.

To succeed in this world, blending in without losing authenticity is important. Strategies include using buzzwords sparingly, mastering the art of redirection to buy time, and appearing engaged through thoughtful nods and occasional contributions. While workplace BS persists because confidence often trumps substance, maintaining genuine contributions when it matters builds trust and credibility. The key is to play the game strategically without becoming consumed by it, ensuring that your value shines in a world powered by polished nonsense.

CHAPTER 19

BULLSHIT IN POP CULTURE

Pop culture is a masterclass in polished nonsense. Everywhere you turn, something shiny, dramatic, and utterly unrealistic is served up for our consumption, and we eagerly indulge. From Hollywood's epic fantasies to influencers' "spontaneous" moments on Instagram, pop culture thrives on illusions we willingly embrace. Let's explore why we're so hooked on these fantasies and how to navigate a world where style often trumps substance.

HOLLYWOOD: THE DREAM MACHINE

Hollywood doesn't just create movies; it creates worlds where the impossible feels plausible. It's the land of slow-motion explosions, flawless heroes, and problems solved with a single training montage. Logic takes a backseat to spectacle, and we happily go along for the ride.

Take action movies. A protagonist survives a car crash, leaps off a building, and takes down ten enemies without breaking a sweat. In real life, a single bad fall would land most of us in the ER. But Hollywood doesn't sell reality; it sells adrenaline-fueled fantasies, and we buy them with popcorn.

Romantic comedies are no better. They turn love into a perfectly scripted fairy tale. Two strangers meet, fall in love within days, and conquer every obstacle before sealing it with a cinematic kiss. Never mind the awkward dates, miscommunications, and laundry piles of real relationships; Hollywood has no patience for mundane realities.

And then there's the classic montage: the magical shortcut to success. Whether learning martial arts or becoming a chess champion, a well-placed montage convinces us that mastery is only a few dramatic minutes away. Meanwhile, the rest of us struggle to assemble IKEA furniture without losing our minds.

The genius of Hollywood lies in its ability to make us believe, if only for a couple of hours. It doesn't matter how absurd the story is. If it makes us feel awe, joy, or excitement, it's done its job.

HOLLYWOOD'S GO-TO TROPES

Pop culture thrives on familiar tropes that suspend disbelief and entertain us despite their absurdity. Here are a few favorites:

The Hacker Genius: Typing furiously, they "crack the code" in seconds, bypassing impenetrable firewalls while shouting, "I'm in!" Hacking involves tedious hours of trial and error, not Hollywood theatrics.

Love at First Sight: A single glance seals the fate of two strangers as soulmates. Real life? It's more "Does this person even text back?" than instant fireworks.

The Invincible Hero: Shot, stabbed, and tossed off a skyscraper, they still deliver a triumphant speech. Let's be honest, a paper cut most of us out of commission.

These tropes don't hold up to scrutiny, but that's not the point. They're designed to delight, not reflect reality. So, the next time you roll your eyes at a hero walking unscathed from an explosion, remember: it's all part of the spectacle.

INSTAGRAM: THE INFLUENCER'S PLAYGROUND

If Hollywood is the master of BS, influencers are its prodigies. They've turned the art of staging perfection into a business model. From sunrise yoga sessions to flawless vacation photos, the influencer illusion is a carefully curated performance.

Consider those dreamy travel posts. Behind the serene beach shot lies a chaotic reality: early mornings, staged poses, and Photoshop magic. And those "effortless" transformation posts? The lighting, angles, and filters are doing most of the work.

Even the simplest moments are fabricated. That "spontaneous" brunch shot? It likely involved 30 minutes of arranging food and chasing perfect lighting. Influencers are selling ideals, not reality. And while we know this, it's hard not to compare our messy, unfiltered lives to their polished feeds.

HOW TO SPOT THE NONSENSE

Pop culture's illusions may be entertaining, but they're easier to spot when you know what to look for:

Excessive Perfection: If it looks too flawless, whether it's a sunset photo or a movie character's life, it's probably staged.

Overuse of Tropes: From hacking montages to whirlwind romances, watch for the over-the-top clichés that scream "fiction."

Context Clues: Pay attention to what's left out. That influencer's "dream vacation" likely involved sweat, stress, and heavy editing.

ENJOY THE SHOW WITHOUT BUYING THE FANTASY

The magic of pop culture lies in its ability to captivate us. Hollywood's blockbusters and Instagram's glossy feeds create escapes from the mundane. But the key to enjoying these illusions is keeping perspective.

Your life doesn't need dramatic montages or picture-perfect moments to be meaningful. The messy, unfiltered, and sometimes boring reality is what makes it uniquely yours. So, laugh at the absurdity, appreciate the artistry, and remind yourself that behind every perfect scene is a lot of editing and a healthy dose of BS.

Pop culture is a kaleidoscope of dazzling illusions; we're all here for the show. Whether it's a hero surviving impossible odds or an influencer's perfect morning routine, it's okay to be entertained. Just don't forget the art of discernment. Behind every cinematic explosion and curated photo lies a lot of BS. So, watch the movie, scroll the feed, and enjoy the spectacle, but remember: your messy, unfiltered life is the ultimate blockbuster.

Pop culture thrives on polished illusions, creating worlds where drama, perfection, and fantasy reign supreme. Hollywood captivates audiences with improbable tropes like invincible heroes, love at first sight, and hacker geniuses who crack complex codes in seconds. These exaggerated narratives, from action-packed blockbusters to romantic comedies, prioritize awe and entertainment over realism. Meanwhile, influencers on Instagram have perfected the art of staging flawless moments, turning travel, fitness, and daily routines into performances of curated perfection. These dreamy snapshots, while captivating, often hide the chaotic and unglamorous reality behind the scenes.

Recognizing the BS in pop culture requires a discerning eye for excessive perfection, clichéd tropes, and what's conveniently left out. While these illusions can inspire and entertain, they should be taken for what they are: escapist fantasies, not reflections of real life. True fulfillment lies in embracing the authenticity of your own messy, unfiltered experiences rather than comparing them to heavily edited ideals. Enjoy the show, but remember, behind every blockbuster or Instagram post is a dose of well-crafted nonsense.

CHAPTER 20

ADVANCED BULLSHIT TECHNIQUES

Congratulations, you've reached the graduate level of BS mastery. This is an elite territory where nonsense transforms from a survival tactic into a strategic skillset. Advanced bullshit isn't for the faint of heart; it's for those moments when you need to dodge blame, buy time, or entertain. If you've ever spun a wildly implausible tale or expertly sidestepped an awkward question, you're already familiar with the basics. Now, let's refine your craft with two essential tools: The Art of Deflection and The Complicated Lie.

THE ART OF DEFLECTION: DODGING ACCOUNTABILITY WITH STYLE

Deflection is the conversational equivalent of a smoke bomb: toss it into a situation and watch the focus shift elsewhere. It's not lying; it's strategic misdirection. If you've ever redirected a tricky question with, "Let's not lose sight of the bigger picture," you've already mastered a key deflection move.

One effective tactic is answering a question with another question. If someone asks, "Why didn't you respond to the email?" instead of admitting you forgot, counter with, "Was it urgent? I didn't get the sense it required immediate action." This technique returns the burden onto them, subtly nudging the spotlight away from your misstep.

Another classic is the subject change. Suppose someone corners you with, "Where's the report you promised?" You reply, "Oh, that reminds me, have you tried the new coffee machine in the breakroom?" They're already thinking about cappuccinos when they realize you've dodged the question. This works best in informal settings, but confidence can carry it further.

The beauty of deflection lies in its subtlety. You're not denying or fabricating anything; you're simply redirecting the conversation. It's a graceful way to sidestep trouble without raising suspicion.

THE COMPLICATED LIE: BALANCING INTRICACY AND PLAUSIBILITY

A complicated lie is an advanced maneuver for situations where simple excuses won't suffice. The trick is providing enough detail to make it believable without overloading the story. Think of it as a tightrope walk between intrigue and overreach.

For instance, if you're late to work, skip the generic "traffic was bad" excuse. Instead, say, "A delivery truck broke down on the main road, rerouting traffic through residential areas. I got stuck behind a moving van trying to back into a driveway." It's specific enough to sound real but simple enough to remember.

However, avoid unnecessary embellishments. Adding extra layers, like, "And then a squirrel chased a cat onto the moving van," risks unraveling your story. Keep it concise, and always ensure your details align. A good, complicated lie is like a movie trailer; it teases enough to intrigue without giving away the plot holes.

Consistency is critical. Forgetting one minor point can expose your fabrication. That's why seasoned bullshitters stick to manageable details that don't require mental gymnastics to keep straight.

CASE STUDIES: WHEN BS BACKFIRES

Even the best bullshitters stumble occasionally. Take Chris, who once claimed his computer crashed to dodge a work deadline. Solid excuse, right? But Chris got carried away, adding that a thunderstorm fried his hard drive, which was encrypted with "top-secret software." When someone asked, "Why didn't you save it to the cloud?" Chris froze, and his elaborate story collapsed faster than a sandcastle at high tide.

Then there's Kelly, who bailed on a dinner party with the excuse of a family emergency involving a broken-down car. Unfortunately, she forgot she'd posted an Instagram story showing her cozy night in with popcorn and a rom-com. Her "emergency" was quickly exposed, and she wasn't invited to the next party.

The lesson? The more intricate the lie, the greater the risk of exposure. Keep it simple, and always consider the possibility of being fact-checked.

MASTERING ADVANCED BS: PRO TIPS

If you're ready to level up your BS game, keep these tips in mind:

Assess the Situation: Not every problem calls for advanced techniques. A straightforward "My bad" is sometimes more effective than a convoluted excuse.

Know Your Audience: Tailor your approach. Buzzwords might impress your boss but will fall flat with friends who know you better.

Simplify Your Story: Overcomplication leads to contradictions. Stick to the essentials, and let your delivery carry the weight.

Sell It with Confidence: Whether you're deflecting or spinning a tale, people will believe you if you sound like you believe in yourself.

THE ART OF STORYTELLING

Advanced bullshit, at its core, is about storytelling. Whether you're redirecting attention in a meeting or weaving a tale of woe about traffic and tech mishaps, the goal is to captivate, not confuse. A well-crafted story doesn't just buy you time or save face; it entertains, amuses, and sometimes even inspires admiration for your creativity.

So, embrace your inner storyteller. Keep it light, keep it sharp, and above all, keep it believable. And when you inevitably stumble (because even pros slip up), laugh it off and enjoy the absurdity. After all, everyone bullshits, it's just a matter of who does it best.

This chapter elevates BS from a mere survival tactic to a refined skill, focusing on two advanced techniques: The Art of Deflection and The Complicated Lie. Deflection, a strategic redirection of attention, is ideal for dodging accountability without outright denial. Tactics like answering a question with another question or changing the subject subtly shift focus, allowing the bullshitter to escape scrutiny. For instance, if asked about a missed deadline, deflect with, "Oh, have you tried the new coffee machine?" Confidence and timing are key to executing this technique effectively.

The Complicated Lie involves crafting detailed yet plausible stories to cover missteps or delays. These lies balance intrigue with believability, offering enough specifics to sound credible without overloading the narrative. For example, blaming tardiness on a traffic jam caused by a delivery truck feels realistic but manageable. However, the chapter warns against overcomplicating lies or forgetting details, as missteps can expose fabrications. Advanced bullshit relies on strong storytelling, audience awareness, and the ability to simplify while maintaining confidence, transforming nonsense into an art form.

CHAPTER 21

LIVING A BULLSHIT-FREE LIFE

Living a bullshit-free life sounds like a utopian dream world where people are upfront, meetings are short, and social media doesn't distort reality. But let's face it: bullshit is everywhere. It's as inevitable as traffic on Monday mornings. The goal isn't to eradicate it (you'd be fighting a losing battle) but to spot it, minimize it, and, most importantly, stop feeding into it.

ESCAPING THE BS TRAP: CALLING YOURSELF OUT

Here's the uncomfortable truth: the person most skilled at bullshitting you is… you. Think about it. How often have you said, "I'll start tomorrow," knowing that tomorrow is a mirage? Or justified procrastination by calling it "research"? These little lies feel harmless until you realize you've built an entire day (or life) around them.

The worst part is you're convincing. "I work better under pressure," you tell yourself as you race to finish a project at 2 a.m., fueled by coffee and panic. Sound familiar? Welcome to the club.

The first step to freedom is identifying your excuses. Write them down whenever you hear yourself say, "I didn't have time," or "This isn't procrastination; it's strategy." Seeing them in black and white makes their absurdity impossible to ignore.

The goal isn't perfection but honesty. Self-awareness is like tidying up a cluttered closet: messy, humbling, and oddly satisfying. And when you're honest with yourself, you'll stop being your own biggest bullshitter.

CUTTING THROUGH ANOTHER PEOPLE'S BS

Navigating others' nonsense is a different challenge. Whether it's a coworker exaggerating their achievements or a friend swearing they were "only five minutes late," their little lies can be exhausting. But you can handle it gracefully.

TECHNIQUES FOR HANDLING NONSENSE

Polite Deflection: A simple "Hmm, interesting" works wonders. It lets the moment pass without confrontation.

Humor as a Shield: When a coworker boasts, "I pulled an all-nighter for that project," you can playfully reply, "And nailed 'Bohemian Rhapsody' at karaoke!" It's lighthearted but effective.

Radical Honesty: Gently challenge the story if the situation calls for it. For example: "Wow, that's impressive. Can you share how you managed it?" This approach works best in professional or high-stakes contexts but requires tact.

RADICAL HONESTY: SIMPLIFYING LIFE

Radical honesty sounds bold: no more lies pretenses, just the truth. But imagine walking into a party and announcing, "I hate small talk, and I'm here for the snacks." Honest? Sure. Socially wise? Maybe not.

Radical honesty isn't about sharing every thought. It's about choosing truth over convenience, even when it's uncomfortable. When someone asks, "How are you?" and you're struggling, you can say, "Not great, but thanks for asking." It's disarming and opens the door to genuine conversation.

The real beauty of radical honesty is freedom. No more juggling half-truths or worrying about being caught in a lie. You might sting a few egos, but the connections you build will be stronger and more authentic.

LIVING BULLSHIT-FREE: FINDING THE BALANCE

Living without bullshit doesn't mean eliminating humor or embellishment. It means using them intentionally. Laugh at silly excuses, enjoy a good story, but don't rely on fluff to avoid reality.

Start small. When you catch yourself making an excuse, pause and ask, "Is this true, or am I avoiding something?" If it's avoidance, face the issue head-on. You'll save time and mental energy in the long run.

Honesty doesn't mean calling out every lie you hear. Sometimes, a nod or a smile is enough. The key is knowing when to let it go and when to set the record straight.

BULLSHIT IN TECHNOLOGY AND THE DIGITAL AGE

Technology has revolutionized our lives, but it's also amplified bullshit. Social media, doctored screenshots, and exaggerated LinkedIn profiles are just a few culprits.

TECH-SAVVY BS

The "Spam Excuse": "Your email went to spam" is the go-to for missed messages. Nobody believes it, but it's hard to disprove.

Inflated Titles: Internships morph into "Executive Director of Operations." LinkedIn, we see you.

Doctored Proof: Photoshop can turn anyone into a social media superstar or "urgent" team player.

NAVIGATING DIGITAL DECEPTION

Social media is the Olympics of bullshit. Carefully curated feeds make lives look flawless while hiding the chaos behind the scenes. That influencer's yacht photo? Probably a rental. The "perfect morning routine"? Four hours of prep for a staged snapshot.

The trick to surviving this digital minefield is skepticism. Look for the cracks, repeated backdrops, suspicious lighting, or overly vague captions. And remember, behind every polished post is a real person with bad hair days, overdue bills, and a messy desktop.

Living a bullshit-free life doesn't mean eliminating nonsense entirely but learning to spot, minimize, and avoid contributing to it. This chapter emphasizes self-awareness as the first step to escaping the

BS trap, particularly the little lies we tell ourselves, like "I'll start tomorrow" or "I work better under pressure." By identifying and confronting these self-deceptions, we can break free from cycles of procrastination and avoidance, leading to a more authentic and productive life.

Handling others' BS involves tactful strategies such as polite deflection, humor, or radical honesty, depending on the context. In the digital age, curated social media feeds and exaggerated profiles amplify the problem. Navigating these illusions requires skepticism and perspective, understanding that the perfection projected online is often staged. Ultimately, living with less BS is about balancing embracing authenticity while using humor and sparingly embellishment. It's about enjoying life's messiness without comparing it to someone else's filtered reality.

FINAL THOUGHTS

Technology and social media thrive on exaggeration. But just because the tools for bullshit are advanced doesn't mean you have to play along. Laugh at the absurdity and appreciate the creativity, but don't compare your reality to someone else's carefully curated façade.

Living a bullshit-free life is less about perfection and more about authenticity. It's about knowing when to laugh off nonsense, speak the truth, and walk away. Because, in the end, life isn't about pretending to have it all figured out; it's about embracing the mess and enjoying the ride.

So, next time someone brags about their "life-changing startup" or posts a too-perfect vacation selfie, smile and nod. They're not fooling anyone, least of all you. After all, the digital age isn't about being perfect; it's about convincing others that you are. And sometimes, the smartest move is not playing the game at all.

CHAPTER 22

SOCIAL MEDIA SMOKE AND MIRRORS

Social media is the magician of the digital age, a master illusionist conjuring a world where everyone seems to have their lives together while secretly Googling "how to feel less like a mess." Platforms like Instagram, TikTok, and Facebook have turned our lives into carefully curated highlight reels. Behind every viral post lies a potent mix of creativity, curation, and, let's face it, an impressive amount of bullshit.

THE ILLUSION OF INFLUENCERS

Influencers reign as the modern aristocracy, blending avocado toast with inspirational captions. Their feeds are packed with snapshots of luxury cars (borrowed), designer outfits (tagged and returned), and blissful routines (meticulously staged). They've built an empire of smoke and mirrors, where even a "casual" photo requires hours of prep, endless retakes, and a parade of filters.

Sponsorships only amplify the illusion. One day, they're touting a protein powder as life-changing; the next, they've switched allegiance to a rival brand. Authenticity? Optional. The goal isn't to use these products but to convince you to buy them. And it works because we crave the fantasy of their perfect lives.

But here's the truth: most influencers are professional bullshitters. Their glamor is a stage, their authenticity an act. Once you realize this, their feeds become less a source of envy and more a spectacle of creative fiction.

CURATED LIFESTYLES: THE HIGHLIGHT REEL

Social media doesn't do "unfiltered." It does a "highlight reel." Your neighbor's breakfast post of an artisan latte and perfectly sliced avocado? It's the product of meticulous staging. Meanwhile, the argument over burnt toast and spilled coffee conveniently didn't make the cut.

Relationships are curated, too. That glowing sunset photo captioned "Forever my person"? It likely followed a spat about who forgot the snacks. Fitness influencers flaunting six-pack abs conveniently omit the hours of editing, restrictive diets, and perfect lighting. Social media isn't where life happens; it's where life is performed.

Next time a post makes you feel like you're falling short, remember: you're seeing the best version of their lives, not the real one. Nobody posts bad days or messy realities because those don't get likes.

VIRAL TRENDS: ABSURDITY IN ACTION

From dance challenges to questionable "life hacks," viral trends are the internet's version of playing follow-the-leader, except the leader is blindfolded and heading toward a cliff. Some trends are harmless fun.

Others, like the Tide Pod or Cinnamon Challenge, leave us collectively questioning humanity.

Even more absurd are the manufactured controversies designed to provoke outrage. Remember the drama over Mr. Potato Head being "canceled"? It was a baseless rumor, yet it ignited a firestorm of debates and clicks. These viral moments thrive on emotional manipulation, making us unwitting participants in someone else's marketing ploy.

The problem? Viral trends exploit our emotions, fear of missing out, desire for approval, and love of a good spectacle. By taking a moment to question their motives, you can avoid falling victim to the madness.

SPOTTING THE BULLSHIT: A SURVIVAL GUIDE

Navigating the jungle of social media requires a sharp BS radar. Here's how to tune yours:

INSPECT THE DETAILS

Photos that seem too perfect often are. Overly smooth skin, glowing sunsets, or pristine workspaces? Likely edited. A reverse image search can even reveal stock photos masquerading as personal content.

QUESTION DRAMATIC CLAIMS

Viral fitness transformations or "spontaneous" dance videos? Often staged. Even sensational headlines are crafted for clicks. Always dig deeper.

TRUST YOUR INSTINCTS

If a post feels off like an influencer hawking a product, they'd never use it, but it probably is. Social media thrives on exaggeration, but a little skepticism goes a long way.

CLOSING REFLECTION

Social media isn't inherently bad; it's a tool. The key is learning to use it without letting it use you. Laugh at the absurdity, question the perfection, and remember that nobody's life is as flawless as their feed suggests. Life happens in the mess, the chaos, and the moments you'd never imagine photographing.

Because let's face it: nobody's reaching for their phone to document laundry piles or burnt toast. And that's okay; just don't let the illusion convince you it's the whole story.

Social media platforms like Instagram and TikTok are modern-day stages for carefully curated highlight reels, where reality is often replaced with illusion. Influencers, the reigning stars of these platforms, create an aura of effortless perfection through staged photos, borrowed luxury, and contradictory sponsorships. Their feeds sell an unattainable fantasy, fostering envy while concealing the behind-the-scenes chaos. Similarly, regular users showcase curated lifestyles that omit mundane or messy realities, presenting relationships, fitness goals, and everyday moments as flawless performances. Social media thrives on these illusions, turning life into staged snapshots rather than authentic experiences.

Viral trends and controversies fuel the social media spectacle, ranging from playful dance challenges to dangerous stunts like the Tide

Pod Challenge. Manufactured outrage over trivial topics, such as the Mr. Potato Head "cancellation," manipulates emotions for clicks and engagement. To navigate this landscape, a sharp BS radar is essential. Inspect overly perfect details, question dramatic claims, and trust your instincts when content feels contrived. Ultimately, social media is a tool, not reality, and by maintaining perspective, you can enjoy its entertainment without succumbing to its illusions. Life's true value lies in the unfiltered moments, not the polished performances.

CHAPTER 23

THE CLICKBAIT CONUNDRUM

SENSATIONAL HEADLINES: THE DIGITAL SIREN SONG

Clickbait is the internet's equivalent of junk food, which is irresistible at the moment but regrettable afterward. Headlines like "You Won't Believe What This Woman Found in Her Backyard!" lure you in with tantalizing promises, only to serve up a slideshow that ends with a raccoon. We've all been there, duped by flashy phrases that prey on our curiosity. Despite knowing better, we click, hoping for a payoff that rarely comes.

What makes these headlines so effective is their ability to manipulate emotions. They tap into curiosity with promises of shocking revelations or trigger fear with urgent warnings like, "Doctors Hate This One Trick!" These emotionally charged hooks bypass our critical thinking, making it hard to resist clicking even when we suspect it's a trap.

But the damage goes beyond wasted time. Sensational headlines often misrepresent facts, spreading misinformation before anyone reads the article. For instance, a headline like "Coffee Causes Cancer!" might bury the nuanced truth "only in lab rats and under extreme conditions" several paragraphs deep. The headline's job isn't to inform; it's to bait you into engaging, leaving misinformation in its wake.

Understanding this tactic is the first step to breaking the cycle. Once you recognize that clickbait is engineered to exploit your impulses, it's easier to pause and question its value. Instead of clicking, take a moment to wonder: "Do I really need to know what's in that backyard?"

FAKE NEWS: LIES DISGUISED AS JOURNALISM

If clickbait is an annoyance, fake news is outright dangerous. Fake news isn't just misleading; it's often a deliberate attempt to deceive and manipulate. Fake news is designed to provoke strong reactions and influence opinions, whether fabricated celebrity scandals or bogus political exposé.

What makes fake news so insidious is its veneer of credibility. It mimics legitimate journalism, with dramatic headlines like "Politician Caught in Shocking Scandal!" or "Scientists Warn of Global Catastrophe!" The goal is to bypass skepticism by looking official, even when the content is pure fiction. These stories are crafted to ignite outrage, fear, or agreement, ensuring they spread rapidly before anyone can verify their claims.

Social media amplifies the problem, turning fake news into a global epidemic. A single fabricated post can reach millions within minutes, thanks to algorithms prioritizing engagement over accuracy. Outrageous lies travel faster than measured truths, leaving confusion and mistrust in their wake. "The Moon Landing Was Faked" will always get more clicks than "NASA Confirms Decades-Old Event."

Combating fake news requires effort from all of us. It's not just about debunking lies; it's about questioning the stories that play to our biases or fears. By approaching sensational claims with skepticism, we can resist becoming unwitting participants in the spread of misinformation.

HOW CLICKBAIT AND FAKE NEWS EXPLOIT EMOTIONS

The secret to clickbait and fake news is emotional manipulation. These tactics exploit our primal curiosity, fear, and outrage instincts to grab attention and drive engagement. Once you understand how they work, you'll see through their tricks and think twice before clicking.

Fear-based headlines are especially effective. Words like "Warning" or "Danger" tap into our survival instincts, compelling us to investigate potential threats. Even when the danger is exaggerated or outright fabricated, we can't help but click. It's the digital equivalent of rubbernecking at a car crash.

Outrage is another emotional lever. Stories that confirm our anger toward specific people, groups, or ideologies spread like wildfire. Headlines designed to provoke indignation don't just validate our feelings; they encourage us to share, creating a feedback loop of misinformation and frustration.

Then there's curiosity, the classic "You Won't Believe What Happens Next!" hook. These headlines exploit our desire for resolution, drawing us in with unanswered questions. But the payoff rarely satisfies, leaving us stuck in a cycle of clicks and disappointment.

Recognizing these emotional triggers helps you reclaim control. Instead of reacting impulsively, pause and consider whether the content is worth your time or if it's just another emotional trap.

STRATEGIES FOR SPOTTING CREDIBLE SOURCES

In the chaos of the digital age, spotting credible sources is a survival skill. It's not about rejecting everything online; it's about navigating the noise with a critical eye. You can separate fact from fiction with a few practical strategies and avoid falling for digital deception.

Start with the source. Reputable outlets are transparent about reporting, citing primary sources, and correcting errors. Suppose a website's name is unfamiliar or sounds more like a meme than a newsroom. In that case, it's worth investigating before taking its claims seriously.

Next, read beyond the headline. Clickbait headlines are designed to mislead, offering sensationalized or incomplete story snapshots. If you do click, pay attention to the tone and structure. Legitimate articles focus on facts, while fake news leans heavily on drama and emotional language.

Verification is crucial. If a story seems outrageous, check if other credible outlets cover it. A lack of corroboration is a red flag. Tools like Snopes and FactCheck.org are invaluable for debunking viral misinformation providing clarity when headlines create confusion.

Finally, trust your instincts. It probably is if a claim feels too good or outrageous to be true. Healthy skepticism isn't cynicism; it's a necessary filter in a world where attention is currency. By staying curious but critical, you can navigate the internet without falling victim to its many traps.

CUTTING THROUGH THE NOISE

Clickbait and fake news thrive on distraction and emotional manipulation, but you don't have to play along. By understanding how they work and adopting a critical approach to online content, you can reclaim your time and mental energy.

The next time a headline promises to change your life, ask yourself: "Do I really need to know this?" Chances are, you don't. Resist the temptation, laugh at the absurdity, and move on. Because in a world full of sensational nonsense, your attention is too valuable to waste.

Clickbait headlines and fake news dominate the digital age, preying on emotions like curiosity, fear, and outrage to drive engagement. Clickbait tempts readers with exaggerated or misleading promises, often leading to underwhelming content that wastes time and spreads misinformation. Headlines like "Doctors Hate This One Trick!" bypass critical thinking by triggering emotional responses. At the same time, fake news goes further, deliberately fabricating stories to deceive, provoke, or manipulate. Social media amplifies these issues by prioritizing virality over accuracy, turning misinformation into a global epidemic.

To navigate this landscape, readers must develop a sharp BS radar and adopt critical strategies to identify credible sources. Checking for reputable outlets, reading beyond sensational headlines, and verifying claims through trusted fact-checking platforms like Snopes are key to combating digital deception. By recognizing emotional triggers and pausing before impulsively clicking, individuals can resist manipulation and reclaim their attention. Ultimately, staying curious but critical allows for a more informed and intentional interaction with online content, cutting through the noise of sensational nonsense.

CHAPTER 24

BATTLING ALGORITHMIC BULLSHIT

THE ALGORITHM: BULLSHIT'S BEST FRIEND

Algorithms are the invisible maestros orchestrating the chaos of the digital world. Sitting silently behind your screen, they decide what you see, from cute cat videos to endless conspiracy theories. They claim to make your life easier, but they're like overeager matchmakers who keep setting you up with "content" you never asked for. If algorithms had a motto, it would likely be, "We know what you want better than you do. Click now!"

At their core, algorithms are engagement machines. They feed off every like, click, and share, doubling down on content that keeps you hooked. Whether it's videos promising "shocking secrets Big Pharma doesn't want you to know" or oddly specific ads for air fryers after one casual Google search, algorithms amplify whatever grabs your attention. Outrage, shock, and curiosity fuel these digital feedback loops, pushing the most outrageous content into the spotlight.

This engagement spiral creates a bizarre ecosystem where a single click on a conspiracy video about ancient aliens can lead to a feed dominated by flat-earth theories and Bigfoot sightings. Algorithms don't care whether the content is true or helpful; they care only about keeping you scrolling. They act as neutral chaos agents, oblivious to the distinction between credible journalism and the ramblings of @FlatEarthGuru69.

While algorithms aren't inherently evil, their unchecked efficiency at promoting nonsense is concerning. They exploit human curiosity and emotions to an almost predatory degree, turning the internet into a playground of half-truths, dubious life hacks, and viral absurdities. The real problem lies not in their existence but in their power to shape perceptions and behaviors without us even realizing it.

WHY OUTRAGE OUTPERFORMS REASON

The success of algorithmic nonsense lies in its exploitation of human psychology. We might like to believe we're rational beings. Still, the truth is that emotional extremes, particularly outrage and shock, grab our attention more effectively than reason ever could. Algorithms know this and leverage it mercilessly.

Outrage, for instance, is incredibly addictive. A provocative comment or an inflammatory headline triggers a surge of adrenaline, pulling us into endless scrolling and heated comment debates. The algorithm interprets this engagement as a green light to serve more of the same, creating a cycle of rage-filled content that's nearly impossible to break.

Shock operates similarly. Headlines like "You Won't Believe What Happened Next!" tap into our innate curiosity, compelling us to click despite knowing we're being manipulated. It's the digital equivalent of peeking into a neighbor's backyard. You're not proud of it, but you can't resist.

Even curiosity itself becomes a tool of manipulation. Posts that hint at "hidden truths" or "exclusive secrets" dangle just enough intrigue to draw us in. Whether or not the content delivers on its promise is irrelevant; the algorithm's goal isn't to inform but to keep you engaged. This exploitation of emotional triggers not only fuels nonsense but makes it harder to focus on meaningful, well-researched content.

Recognizing these tactics is the first step in fighting back. Once you know how algorithms manipulate your emotions, you can approach online content with skepticism and self-control, breaking the cycle of outrage and shock that keeps nonsense thriving.

THE NONSENSE AVALANCHE

One of the most dangerous aspects of algorithmic bullshit is its ability to snowball. A single click or share can transform minor nonsense into a full-blown internet phenomenon, thanks to algorithms amplifying attention-grabbing content without regard for its quality or consequences.

Take viral challenges as a prime example. Remember the Tide Pod Challenge? It began as a joke but escalated into a global trend with real-world consequences, including hospital visits. Why? Because algorithms recognized the high engagement and decided it was exactly what everyone needed to see. Public health concerns were irrelevant; what mattered was that people couldn't stop watching.

Even seemingly innocuous trends aren't immune. A simple post about minimalist living can balloon into an entire aesthetic movement, with overpriced "minimalist" products and influencers showing off their "simple" lifestyles on Instagram. The algorithm doesn't distinguish between genuine enthusiasm and fleeting curiosity; it promotes whatever generates clicks, likes, and shares.

This avalanche effect also applies to misinformation. A baseless conspiracy theory can quickly gain momentum, spreading from obscure forums to mainstream feeds. The more people engage with it, whether to agree, debunk, or mock it, the more the algorithm pushes it into the spotlight. This self-perpetuating cycle makes it nearly impossible to contain the spread of nonsense once it gains traction.

The speed of this amplification is what makes it so dangerous. Misinformation or absurdity can dominate the digital conversation within hours, influencing opinions and decisions before facts catch up. Understanding how this avalanche works is crucial to navigating the internet without getting buried under its weight.

HOW TO OUTSMART THE ALGORITHM

Algorithms may be relentless, but they're not invincible. With mindful practices and a critical eye, you can take control of your digital experience and minimize the influence of algorithmic nonsense. It's about reclaiming your power as a user, not abandoning the internet altogether.

- **Curate Your Feed Intentionally**

    Algorithms are powered by your interactions, so be deliberate about what you engage with. Avoid clicking on sensational headlines or commenting on provocative posts, even if you disagree. Instead, like, share, and interact with thoughtful, educational, or genuinely enjoyable content. Over time, the algorithm will adapt to these preferences, showing you more of what you value.

- **Follow Credible Sources**

    Seek out reputable accounts and pages that prioritize accuracy over sensationalism. Verified experts, established news outlets and reliable science communicators are excellent starting points. While their headlines may not be as flashy, their content will be far more trustworthy.

- **Avoid Trolls and Outrage Bait**

    Resist the temptation to engage with inflammatory posts or comments. Even negative engagement boosts visibility, encouraging the algorithm to promote such content further. Instead, block, mute, or report offending accounts and move on.

- **Take Digital Breaks**

    Stepping away from social media periodically can do wonders for your mental clarity. The less time you spend online, the less influence algorithms have over your thoughts and behaviors. Use these breaks to reconnect with offline activities that bring you joy and perspective.

RECLAIMING YOUR DIGITAL SPACE

In a world where algorithms shape much of what we see and believe, it's easy to feel like a passive participant in the chaos. But you have more control than you realize. By being intentional about your online habits and questioning the content you encounter, you can reduce the impact of algorithmic nonsense and foster a healthier digital environment.

Think of your digital space as a garden without regular pruning; weeds will overrun it. Engage with content that inspires, informs, or entertains you meaningfully. Don't hesitate to unfollow accounts that contribute to negativity or misinformation. The algorithm is powerful, but it's also predictable, and with the right strategies, you can outsmart it.

Above all, remember to approach the internet with humor and perspective. Algorithms may be frustrating, but they're also hilariously bad at nuance. Laugh at the absurdity, share a meme, and don't forget that the messy, unpredictable, and gloriously algorithm-free real world is still out there waiting for you.

Algorithms dominate the digital landscape, feeding users content that maximizes engagement rather than quality or truth. Designed to amplify attention-grabbing material, algorithms exploit emotional triggers like outrage, shock, and curiosity to keep users scrolling, regardless of whether the content is credible or helpful. This creates a feedback loop where even a single interaction with sensational material can snowball into an avalanche of nonsense dominating your feed. Viral challenges, misleading trends, and misinformation thrive in this environment, often spreading faster than corrections or facts can catch up.

To combat algorithmic manipulation, users must proactively reclaim their digital spaces. Strategies include curating feeds by engaging only with trustworthy content, avoiding inflammatory posts that fuel engagement, and following credible sources. Taking regular breaks from social media helps regain clarity and reduces the influence of these digital systems. While algorithms aren't inherently malicious, their unchecked power can distort perceptions and behaviors. By fostering skepticism and intentional online habits, individuals can reduce the noise, laugh at the absurdities, and cultivate a healthier relationship with technology.

CHAPTER 25

ROMANTIC BULLSHIT

Romantic relationships are fertile ground for a unique kind of bullshit: a mix of charm, theatrics, and the occasional stretch of the truth. From playful exaggerations to relationship-damaging deceptions, romantic bullshit ranges from harmless to catastrophic. It's often used to maintain harmony, avoid conflict, or add flair to the mundane. But where's the line between endearing white lies and relationship-sinking deceptions? Let's explore the spectrum of romantic bullshit sprinkled with humor and a dose of practical wisdom.

THE HARMLESS LIES THAT KEEP LOVE ALIVE

Not all lies are created equal. In fact, some lies serve as the glue holding relationships together during rough patches. These white lies are the verbal equivalent of a Band-Aid: quick fixes to smooth over minor issues, often told with good intentions.

Think of the classic, "I love your cooking!" when your partner's culinary experiment is one step away from biohazard status. Or the ubiquitous, "Of course, I noticed your haircut!" which is shorthand for, "I noticed it just now when you mentioned it." These lies are not about deceit but about preserving the small joys of daily life, like enthusiasm or confidence.

Then there's the perennial favorite: "I'm fine." These words can mean anything from "I'm mildly annoyed" to "I'm silently reliving that argument we had in 2014." While these small fibs might seem harmless, they tend to pile up. Pretending to enjoy karaoke or feigning interest in a hobby you secretly loathe might stave off a disagreement. Still, it can lead to resentment over time. A little white lie here, and it is fine. Just don't let it replace genuine communication.

THE DAMAGING DECEPTIONS THAT SINK RELATIONSHIPS

At the other end of the spectrum lie the heavy hitters, the deceptions that erode trust and can shatter even the strongest relationships. These aren't the "I forgot to take out the trash" kind of lies; they're the ones that leave emotional scars.

Infidelity, financial dishonesty, and the all-too-common "I'm busy with work" excuse (when they're clearly not) are prime examples of destructive lies. These deceptions don't just create cracks in a relationship; they dynamite its foundation. Once trust is broken, rebuilding it requires immense effort, vulnerability, and time.

Why do people tell these lies? Often, it's rooted in fear, fear of confrontation, fear of losing their partner, or fear of facing their own failures. In other cases, it's simple selfishness. Regardless of the motivation, the outcome is the same: emotional disorientation, a communication breakdown, and a relationship on shaky ground. Addressing such betrayals requires honesty, accountability, and a willingness to converse toughly. Without these, even the sincerest apologies won't repair the damage.

BUILDING TRUST WITHOUT SACRIFICING HUMOR

Healthy relationships thrive on a balance of honesty, trust, and humor. Transparency doesn't mean airing every fleeting thought but being upfront about your feelings, priorities, and mistakes. Vulnerability may feel uncomfortable, but it's essential for true connection. Admitting to accidentally shrinking their favorite sweater might sting at the moment, but it builds trust for tackling bigger issues.

Humor, too, is a powerful tool for navigating the messy realities of romance. Owning it with a playful twist can go a long way when you inevitably mess up. "I forgot our anniversary because I'm an idiot who doesn't deserve you" is far more endearing than defensiveness. Laughter reminds you both that you're on the same team, even when things go wrong.

Honesty doesn't mean brutal candor. For example, if your partner asks, "Do I look okay in this outfit?" and the answer isn't a resounding yes, there's always a diplomatic way to respond. "That other outfit you tried on really brought out your eyes" conveys honesty while preserving their confidence. Balance is key; kindness and truth don't have to be at odds.

NAVIGATING BULLSHIT IN THE DIGITAL AGE

Modern technology has brought a new dimension to romantic bullshit. Social media, dating apps, and text messaging have made it easier to curate idealized versions of ourselves and, unfortunately, to obscure the truth. Whether it's the art of "breadcrumbing" (sending just enough messages to keep someone hooked) or ghosting (the ultimate act of avoidance), digital communication has given rise to new forms of romantic nonsense.

Social media is another playground for curated deception. Carefully staged Instagram posts of "perfect" relationships often mask real struggles. Text messages like "Sorry, I didn't see your text" (when you clearly did) create unnecessary friction. Navigating this landscape requires clear communication and established boundaries. Flirting online might feel harmless to one partner and like a betrayal to another. Discuss expectations early to avoid misunderstandings.

For those braving the dating world, trust your instincts. If someone always seems "too busy" to meet up but has time for gym selfies, they're not prioritizing you. Walk away with your self-respect intact and your bullshit radar sharpened.

THE FINE ART OF ROMANTIC BULLSHIT

Romantic bullshit is part of the human experience. A little white lie used sparingly and with good intentions, can keep the peace and add charm to a relationship. But too much or the wrong kind can erode trust and connection. The secret lies in knowing when to sprinkle bullshit and when to be unapologetically honest.

The good news? Love is resilient. With open communication, a sense of humor, and mutual respect, you can navigate the ups and downs of romance without succumbing to nonsense. And if all else fails, remember: a well-timed joke can diffuse almost any tension. After all, laughter is the glue that holds even the messiest relationships together.

Romantic relationships are rife with bullshit, ranging from harmless white lies to damaging deceptions. Playful exaggerations like "I love your cooking" or "I'm fine" often serve to maintain harmony and avoid unnecessary conflict. While these small fibs can smooth over rough patches, they may also accumulate and hinder genuine communication if overused. On the other hand, destructive lies such as infidelity, financial dishonesty, or habitual excuses can erode trust and dismantle even strong relationships. Rebuilding from such betrayals demands vulnerability, accountability, and open dialogue.

In today's digital age, technology has amplified romantic bullshit through dating apps, social media, and curated online personas. Practices like "breadcrumbing" or "ghosting" and staged social media posts of seemingly perfect relationships create additional layers of deception. Successfully navigating these challenges requires trust, clear boundaries, and honest communication. While a touch of romantic bullshit can add charm, the key to healthy relationships lies in balancing honesty, humor, and respect. Ultimately, love thrives on mutual understanding, trust, and the ability to laugh together through life's imperfections.

CHAPTER 26

BULLSHIT AT WORK

The workplace is fertile ground for nonsense, where buzzwords, office politics, and exaggerated egos flourish like weeds in an untended garden. From overly polished corporate emails to the unspoken games of power and influence, navigating this landscape requires humor, awareness, and patience. But fear not. With a strategic approach, you can sidestep the pitfalls of professional bullshit and thrive amidst the chaos.

Workplace communication is often a masterclass in saying a lot without saying anything. Over time, plain language has replaced jargon-heavy phrases designed to confuse rather than clarify. Words like "synergy," "leverage," and "disruption" are staples of this nonsense orchestra, leaving employees to decipher their meaning while suppressing an eye roll.

Take the phrase "Let's circle back." It sounds proactive but often means, "I don't have an answer, so let's talk about it later and hope someone else figures it out." Or the ever-present "Think outside the box," usually uttered by someone who couldn't locate the box with a GPS. These phrases create an illusion of progress while expertly avoiding accountability.

The real virtuosos of buzzwords can craft sentences that sound impressive but devoid of substance. For instance, "We need to leverage core competencies to achieve strategic alignment." Translation? "I'm hoping this string of buzzwords will mask the fact that I have no clear plan."

To combat this, call out the absurdity with humor and clarity. If someone says, "Let's ideate around this issue," respond with, "Great, let's start by defining ideate." A well-timed laugh can remind everyone that plain language is more effective and far less pretentious.

THE GAME OF OFFICE POLITICS

Office politics is the unspoken drama that plays out in every workplace. It's less about job titles and more about who has it, who wants it, and who's willing to bend the rules to get it. Power dynamics bring out the best and worst in people, leading to behavior that ranges from mildly irritating to outright Machiavellian.

Key players in this game include the Overpromise, who guarantees results they can't deliver, and the Passive-Aggressive Emailer, whose subject lines like "Quick Follow-Up :)" carry an undertone of barely concealed frustration. Then there's the Office Gossip, whose main function seems to be circulating half-truths and drama faster than a Slack notification.

Navigating this minefield requires diplomacy and self-awareness. First, identify the players and their motives. Understanding who's in it for power versus those simply trying to survive helps you plan your interactions. Next, document everything: emails, contributions, and decisions. Receipts are invaluable when faced with workplace nonsense.

Finally, stay out of unnecessary drama. If tensions escalate, play the role of the neutral diplomat: "I didn't realize this was such a hot topic; let's focus on the agenda."

The key is to maintain professionalism while keeping a safe distance from politics. Choose your battles wisely, and remember that sometimes, the best move is no move.

CO-WORKERS WHO OVERSELL THEMSELVES

Every office has that one colleague whose confidence far outweighs their competence. They're the self-proclaimed visionaries, constantly making grand claims about their achievements while contributing little substance. These individuals are masters of overpromising and underdelivering, leaving their coworkers to pick up the slack.

Take the Meeting Maverick, who always has something to say but rarely anything meaningful. "We need to align our goals with the broader strategic vision," they announce as if unlocking the universe's secrets. Meanwhile, their actual contributions remain as vague as their statements.

Then there's the Workplace Magician, who vanishes as deadlines approach, only reappearing at the last moment to take credit for the team's work. "This was such a collaborative effort," they'll declare, implying they orchestrated the project when, in reality, they barely showed up.

To handle these types, focus on visibility and accountability. Keep a clear record of your contributions, and don't shy away from asserting your role in team successes. For example, in meetings, say, "To build on my earlier point..." or "As we discussed last week..." to subtly but effectively remind others of your input. And when dealing with credit-stealers, maintain professionalism while firmly reclaiming what's yours: "I'm glad Greg highlighted that it ties back to the draft I shared earlier."

STRATEGIES FOR MANAGING WORKPLACE BULLSHIT

Dealing with workplace nonsense doesn't mean resigning yourself to frustration. You can manage the chaos and maintain your sanity with smart strategies.

- **Master the Art of Deflection**

    When someone tries to pull you into unnecessary drama, deflect with grace. "That's an interesting thought! Let's revisit it after tackling today's priorities." It's polite and professional and keeps you focused on what matters.

- **Set Boundaries**

    Boundaries are essential for maintaining your mental well-being. If a coworker routinely offloads their work onto you, learn to say no tactfully. "I'm currently at capacity with my own deadlines but happy to assist once I wrap this up."

- **Use Humor Wisely**

    Humor can be a powerful tension diffuser. A lighthearted comment can shift the mood without escalating conflict if someone's suggestion or behavior borders on the absurd. "That's an ambitious plan. Have you considered pitching it to Netflix?"

- **Find Your Allies**

   Identify colleagues who share your work ethic and values. These allies can provide support, a sounding board for frustrations, or even a shared laugh over the latest office absurdity.

- **Don't Take It Home**

   Leave workplace nonsense at the office. When you clock out, focus on activities that bring you joy and relaxation. The drama will still be there tomorrow, but your time off is precious.

- **Thriving Amid Workplace Chaos**

   The workplace will never be free of bullshit; it's part of the fabric of professional life. But with humor, self-awareness, and a clear strategy, you can navigate even the most nonsense-filled environments without losing your cool.

   Next time someone suggests "circling back to align on strategic priorities," smile and nod, knowing you've cracked the code to surviving and thriving in the bullshit circus. Remember, nonsense may be inevitable, but how you respond to it is entirely up to you. Keep your sense of humor intact and your focus sharp. You've got this.

   Workplaces are fertile ground for nonsense, from jargon-filled communication to manipulative office politics. Buzzwords like "synergy" or phrases like "Let's circle back" create an illusion of productivity while masking a lack of substance. Similarly, office politics involve power plays, passive-aggressive emails, and gossip that can derail collaboration. Navigating this environment requires humor, clarity, and diplomacy. Calling out confusing jargon with a touch of humor or documenting your contributions to maintain accountability are effective tactics to counter workplace BS.

Coworkers who oversell themselves or take undue credit are a common challenge. To manage them, focus on visibility, reinforce your contributions in discussions, and maintain professional boundaries. Strategies such as deflecting drama, setting limits on extra work, and using humor to diffuse tension can help you thrive amidst the chaos. Additionally, finding workplace allies and leaving work-related frustrations at the office can ensure a healthier balance. While professional nonsense may never disappear, a mix of wit, awareness, and strategic thinking can help you maintain your sanity and succeed in any work environment.

CHAPTER 27

THE CHARISMATIC BULLSHITTER

Leadership can be an incredible force for good, inspiring people to strive for greatness. But it also provides fertile ground for the charismatic bullshitter, an individual whose charm, persuasive rhetoric, and knack for storytelling can rally teams, even if the destination is a dead end. This chapter explores the fine line between inspiration and manipulation, arming you with the tools to discern genuine leadership from smoke and mirrors.

THE ART OF STORYTELLING: INSPIRING WITH A DASH OF BS

Great leaders know that cold, hard facts rarely ignite passion. Data points and spreadsheets might inform, but they seldom inspire. Enter storytelling, a powerful tool that connects emotionally and creates a sense of shared purpose. Charismatic leaders craft narratives that make even mundane objectives sound like epic missions.

Consider the CEO who reminisces about starting their business in a garage with nothing but "grit and determination." The truth? It was a three-car garage in their parents' mansion. The embellishment may be glaring, but the emotional impact is undeniable. It's not the garage that matters; it's the struggle, resilience, and triumph that people connect with.

These stories can motivate teams, build loyalty, and foster unity when used responsibly. They become a rallying cry, like a coach's halftime speech, galvanizing people to achieve more than they thought possible. However, the line between storytelling and manipulation is thin. When leaders twist facts, inflate their achievements, or omit crucial details, their charisma becomes a tool for deception rather than inspiration.

The key to navigating this dynamic is discernment. A leader who uses storytelling as a motivational tool is an asset. One who uses it to obscure the truth or inflate their ego? That's where the bullshit begins to stink.

WHEN CHARISMA TURNS TO MANIPULATION

Charisma is a double-edged sword. In the right hands, it inspires. In the wrong hands, it manipulates. What begins as a rousing speech can quickly morph into guilt trips, gaslighting, or unrealistic demands.

Manipulative leaders use their charm to distort reality for personal gain. They might frame team failures as collective shortcomings, conveniently omitting their role in setting unattainable goals. "If only we had worked harder," they lament, conveniently deflecting accountability.

Another hallmark of manipulation is faux empowerment. They'll say, "I believe in you," while offloading the most challenging tasks with little support, framing it as a "growth opportunity." The result? You feel flattered yet exploited, juggling responsibilities that should have been shared.

Fear-based tactics are another favorite weapon. By hinting that job security or the company's future hangs in the balance, manipulative leaders create an environment of pressure and compliance. If their pep talks leave you feeling more anxious than inspired, it's a red flag worth paying attention to.

Recognizing these behaviors is crucial. While genuine leaders use charisma to uplift, manipulative ones exploit it to serve their agendas. Differentiating between the two can save you from being drawn into their nonsense web.

SPOTTING THE CHARISMATIC BULLSHITTER

Identifying a charismatic bullshitter isn't always easy after all; charm can be blinding. However, there are distinct traits that can help you separate genuine leadership from theatrics.

- **The Substance Test**

    Does their message have actionable content, or is it all flair? True leaders present clear plans, measurable goals, and meaningful steps. Bullshitters rely on vague platitudes like "Let's innovate for success" without defining what innovation entails.

- **Accountability**

    Observe how they handle setbacks. Genuine leaders own their mistakes and actively work to resolve them. Manipulative ones shift blame, often targeting the team they're supposed to support.

- **Consistency**

    Words mean little without corresponding actions. If a leader preaches transparency but makes decisions in secrecy, their charisma might be a cover for deeper issues.

- **Impact on Morale**

    Take note of how their leadership affects the team. Do their words leave you feeling empowered and valued or uncertain and drained? The latter often signals a bullshitter at work.

Once you've identified a charismatic bullshitter, you have options: confront the behavior, work around it with a strategic smile, or start updating your resume. Regardless of your choice, grounding yourself in facts and reality is essential.

USING CHARISMA FOR GOOD: A GUIDE FOR LEADERS

Charisma isn't inherently bad. When used with integrity, it can inspire teams, foster loyalty, and drive success. Here's how leaders can wield charisma responsibly:

- **Be Authentic**

    Authenticity is the foundation of trust. If your stories aren't rooted in genuine experience, they'll appear hollow. People connect with honesty, not theatrics.

- **Ground Stories in Reality**

    Feel free to embellish for impact, but don't stray into fiction. If your tales start resembling a superhero origin story, it's time to pull back. People want relatable leaders, not mythological figures.

- **Empower, Don't Exploit**

    Empowerment means providing tools and support, not overloading your team and calling it growth. Ensure your team feels valued for their contributions, not used for your convenience.

- **Own Your Mistakes**

    Acknowledging errors demonstrates humility and accountability. It humanizes you, making it easier for your team to respect and trust your leadership.

True leadership balances charisma with honesty and integrity. By staying grounded and genuine, you can inspire without resorting to manipulation and earn the respect of those you lead.

CHARISMA WITH A CONSCIENCE

The charismatic bullshitter is a compelling figure equal parts motivator, magician, and opportunist. While their charm can inspire, it can also mislead. Whether dealing with one or trying to avoid becoming one, the key is recognizing charisma's power and wielding it responsibly.

Leadership is about more than dazzling speeches and grand promises. It's about trust, authenticity, and empowering others to achieve their best. The next time someone promises to "disrupt the industry with game-changing innovation," take a step back and ask: is this vision just a pile of well-packaged nonsense?

And if it's the latter? Keep your sense of humor intact, and don't be afraid to question it because nothing disarms a charismatic bullshitter like a well-placed dose of reality served with a smile.

Charismatic leaders use storytelling and charm to inspire teams, connecting emotionally and fostering shared purpose. While these qualities can motivate and unite, they blur the line between inspiration and manipulation. A genuine leader uses narratives to galvanize action and build trust. In contrast, a manipulative one distorts facts, deflects blame, and exploits team members under the guise of empowerment. Recognizing these approaches' differences involves evaluating their substance, accountability, consistency, and impact on morale.

To wield charisma responsibly, leaders must balance their charm with authenticity, grounding their stories in reality and empowering rather than exploiting their teams. Acknowledging mistakes and supporting their team fosters trust and respect. Leadership driven by integrity and honesty turns charisma into a force for good, ensuring it inspires rather than misleads. For followers, discerning between visionary leadership and theatrics helps maintain perspective and confidently navigate workplace dynamics.

CHAPTER 28

LEADING WITHOUT LYING

Leadership is often a balancing act; a tightrope walks over a sea of buzzwords, fragile egos, and looming deadlines. But what if leadership didn't require a reliance on polished half-truths or overblown promises? Imagine a world where you could guide and inspire your team through clarity, authenticity, and trust, no bullshit required. This chapter dives into the allure of nonsense in leadership and how to lead effectively without it, delivering results that are as genuine as they are impactful.

THE ALLURE OF BULLSHIT IN LEADERSHIP

Let's address the obvious: why do so many leaders lean on bullshit? It's often seen as a shortcut to smooth over uncomfortable realities or rally the troops with grandiose promises. It's tempting because it feels like armor, protecting leaders from admitting they don't have all the answers.

Bullshit allows leaders to reframe problems with euphemisms like "strategic pivot" instead of "we made a mistake" or declare "we're exploring innovative solutions" when no concrete plan exists. While this approach might buy short-term buy-in, it comes at a steep cost: trust erosion. Teams quickly pick up on the disconnect between rhetoric and reality, leading to disengagement, cynicism, and a loss of credibility.

To break free from the nonsense cycle, leaders must embrace honesty, not brutal, unfiltered truth, but thoughtful transparency that builds trust and fosters loyalty.

TRANSPARENCY: THE BEDROCK OF TRUST

Transparency isn't about revealing every detail or turning leadership into a confessional. It's about clarity, context, and honesty qualities that transform uncertainty into collaboration.

- **Clarity Is Key**

  People can't follow a leader if they don't understand the direction. Vague statements like "the future is uncertain" sow confusion, while clear communication reassures. Instead, say: "We're facing challenges, but here's what we're doing to address them." Clarity helps teams feel grounded, even when the road ahead is bumpy.

- **Context Creates Understanding**

  Decisions that seem baffling in isolation often make sense when explained. For instance, if budgets need tightening, don't announce cuts without explanation. Share the reasoning: "We're reallocating resources to prepare for potential shifts in the market." Context fosters cooperation and reduces fear.

- **Honesty Earns Respect**

  Leaders who admit when they don't have all the answers or own up to mistakes build stronger connections with their teams. Statements like, "We underestimated the timeline, but here's how we'll adjust," demonstrate accountability and relatability. Honesty isn't a weakness; it's a bridge to trust.

By prioritizing transparency, leaders can transform uncertainty into confidence and doubt into shared purpose.

AUTHENTICITY: YOUR LEADERSHIP SUPERPOWER

Authenticity is the secret sauce that turns trust into loyalty. Authentic leaders don't project perfection; they embrace their humanity, quirks, and limitations. They connect on a deeper level because they're real.

- **Start with Self-Awareness**

  Authenticity begins with knowing yourself. Understand your strengths and weaknesses, and don't pretend to be something you're not. If public speaking isn't your forte, own it. "I'm more comfortable with one-on-one conversations, but I'll give this my best shot" is far more relatable than a forced display of confidence.

- **Build Personal Connections**

  Authentic leaders invest in their teams beyond the task list. A simple "How's your son's baseball team?" shows you see your employees as people, not just roles. Genuine curiosity about their lives fosters goodwill and strengthens relationships.

- **Consistency in Values**

  Authenticity isn't just about being relatable; it's about aligning your actions with your words. If you champion work-life balance, don't send late-night emails or schedule last-minute meetings. Walking the talk earns respect and inspires others to follow your example.

Authenticity is contagious. When leaders show up as their true selves, they encourage their teams to do the same, creating an environment of mutual trust and respect.

PRACTICAL STRATEGIES FOR NO-BS LEADERSHIP

The philosophy of bullshit-free leadership is great, but how do you put it into action? Here are five strategies to lead with integrity and authenticity:

- **Speak Plainly**

    Ditch jargon for clear, straightforward language. Instead of saying, "We're leveraging synergies to optimize our verticals," try, "Let's figure out how to work better together." Simplicity fosters understanding.

- **Own Your Mistakes**

    Mistakes happen; it's how you handle them that matters. Acknowledge errors quickly and outline a plan to address them. "I misjudged this situation, and here's what we'll do to fix it." This not only rebuilds trust but also sets a powerful example.

- **Celebrate Progress**

    Recognize small wins instead of waiting for perfection. Celebrating milestones keeps morale high and reminds your team that their efforts matter.

- **Set Realistic Expectations**

    Overpromising leads to disappointment. Be honest about what's achievable and deliver on your commitments. Teams respect leaders who are grounded in reality.

- **Create Safe Spaces**

    Foster an environment where team members feel heard and valued. Encourage open dialogue, ask for feedback, and genuinely listen to their concerns. When people feel safe, they're more engaged and willing to contribute.

THE PAYOFF: LOYALTY, ENGAGEMENT, AND RESULTS

Leading without bullshit isn't just ethical, it's effective. Teams that trust their leaders are more innovative, resilient, and motivated. They don't just comply; they commit. The result is a workplace where people feel valued, supported, and inspired to do their best.

But make no mistake: bullshit-free leadership takes courage. It requires owning up to uncomfortable truths, admitting vulnerabilities, and fostering open dialogue. The rewards, loyalty, respect, and meaningful impact make it all worthwhile.

THE NO-BS LEADERSHIP MANIFESTO

Bullshit-free leadership is both a challenge and an opportunity. It's about rejecting the temptation to spin facts, embracing transparency, and leading authentically. Leaders who choose this path stand out in a world saturated with empty promises and performative rhetoric.

So, ditch the buzzwords, skip the spin, and show up as the real you. Lead with integrity, foster trust, and create a culture where people are inspired to follow, not because they're dazzled, but because they believe in you.

Ultimately, real leadership isn't about how good you sound; it's about how much you care and the difference you make. And that's a legacy worth leaving.

Leadership often falls prey to polished half-truths and exaggerated promises, but true effectiveness comes from clarity, authenticity, and trust. The allure of bullshit in leadership lies in its perceived ability to smooth over challenges or rally teams with grandiose promises. However, this approach erodes trust and fosters cynicism. Breaking the cycle requires embracing thoughtful transparency, where leaders provide clarity, context, and honesty without overwhelming their teams with unnecessary detail.

Authenticity is a leader's superpower, turning trust into loyalty. Leaders create genuine bonds with their teams by being self-aware, building personal connections, and staying consistent with their values. Practical strategies for no-BS leadership include speaking plainly, owning mistakes, celebrating progress, setting realistic expectations, and creating safe spaces for open dialogue. These practices inspire teams to commit fully, driving innovation and resilience.

Leading without nonsense is both a challenge and an opportunity. It takes courage to reject spin, admit vulnerabilities, and prioritize integrity. Yet, the rewards of a loyal, engaged, and inspired team make it worth the effort. In a world filled with empty promises, leaders who lead with authenticity leave a meaningful and lasting legacy.

CHAPTER 29

FOLLOWING THE BULLSHITTER

THE FINE LINE BETWEEN INSPIRATION AND MANIPULATION

Leadership bullshit runs the gamut from harmless exaggeration to full-blown manipulation. On one side, there's the feel-good fluff that lifts spirits during rough patches. On the other, the calculated nonsense confuses teams and erodes trust. The challenge lies in deciphering whether your leader's motivational speech is a genuine rallying cry or a polished distraction.

Harmless inspirational nonsense often has a purpose. A leader might share a slightly embellished tale of perseverance to encourage resilience. Maybe their story of "starting from nothing" skips over a trust fund or two, but the underlying message that hard work pays off resonates. These stories, while exaggerated, aim to motivate rather than deceive.

On the flip side, manipulative bullshit exploits emotions for personal gain. Think promises of "groundbreaking opportunities" that never materialize or vague declarations like, "This project will redefine our industry," delivered without any actionable plans. This rhetoric may sound inspiring initially but often leaves employees disoriented and disheartened.

The easiest way to tell the difference? Pay attention to how you feel afterward. Inspirational nonsense energizes and excites. Manipulative nonsense leaves you confused, skeptical, or drained. If every meeting feels like a performance devoid of substance, it's time to scrutinize your leader's intentions.

RED FLAGS: HOW TO SPOT DANGEROUS BULLSHIT

Not all leadership nonsense is created equal, and recognizing the signs of manipulative rhetoric can save you frustration and wasted energy. Here's what to look for:

- **Overuse of Buzzwords**

  Leaders who string together jargon like "synergize scalable solutions" or "disruptive innovations" often prioritize sounding impressive over being clear. Take note if their speeches feel like a word salad with no dressing.

- **Lack of Accountability**

  Watch how your leader handles setbacks. A manipulative leader will blame "external factors" or call failures "learning opportunities" while deflecting responsibility. On the flip side, successes are always theirs to claim.

- **Relentless Positivity**

  Optimism is great, but when it ignores reality, it becomes dangerous. Leaders promising "unprecedented growth" while slashing budgets or imposing impossible deadlines are selling a fantasy, not a strategy.

- **Empty Promises**

    Suppose your leader frequently announces "game-changing" initiatives that never deliver. In that case, it's a sign they may be more focused on appearances than outcomes.

Spotting these patterns early allows you to set boundaries, manage expectations, and protect yourself from unnecessary chaos.

WHEN (AND HOW) TO CALL OUT BULLSHIT

Calling out leadership nonsense is a delicate art. Done well, it can redirect focus and improve team dynamics. If done poorly, it can cause tension or damage your professional reputation.

- **Pick Your Battles**

    Not every exaggeration or buzzword is worth addressing. Ask yourself, "Is this rhetoric misleading or just mildly annoying?" Save your energy for instances that genuinely impact the team or project outcomes.

- **Focus on the Message, Not the Messenger**

    Critique ideas, not people. Instead of saying, "This plan is ridiculous," try, "I'm concerned about the feasibility of this timeline given our current resources." Framing feedback constructively reduces defensiveness.

- **Use Questions to Highlight Gaps**

    Questions can expose the cracks in a leader's rhetoric without directly challenging them. For instance, if they claim, "This strategy will revolutionize our industry," ask, "What specific steps will we take to achieve this?"

- **Choose the Right Setting**

    Publicly calling out nonsense can backfire, especially if it embarrasses your leader. Address concerns privately whenever possible. A respectful, one-on-one conversation is more likely to yield productive results.

    By approaching these moments with tact and thoughtfulness, you can push for clarity and accountability without creating unnecessary friction.

HOW TO FOLLOW A BULLSHITTER WITHOUT LOSING YOUR MIND

Sometimes, following a leader prone to nonsense isn't optional. Whether they're your boss or just the loudest voice in the room, navigating their rhetoric without losing your sanity is a vital skill.

- **Ground Yourself in Your Values**

    Don't let their rhetoric derail your integrity. Stay focused on your principles and let them guide your actions. When their speeches sound like motivational gibberish, remind yourself that your work has its own meaning.

- **Translate Rhetoric into Action**

    If their instructions are vague or overly idealistic, break them into practical tasks. For example, if they say, "Let's disrupt the status quo," interpret it as "We need a fresh approach time to brainstorm ideas."

- **Find Humor in the Absurdity**

    Sometimes, the best way to cope with nonsense is to laugh at it. Share a knowing look with colleagues, create a bingo card of their favorite buzzwords, or privately joke about their latest over-the-top declarations.

- **Focus on the Bigger Picture**

  Even if their style grates on you, remember that the team's goals often matter more than the leader's methods. Stay committed to the mission and use their rhetoric as fuel to clarify what truly needs to be done.

You can navigate their nonsense by staying grounded, proactive, and lighthearted without letting it derail your progress.

THRIVING DESPITE THE BULLSHIT

Following a leader prone to nonsense doesn't mean surrendering to it. By recognizing the difference between harmless inspiration and harmful manipulation, you can maintain your focus and sanity. Whether you're translating vague instructions into action, diplomatically challenging flawed ideas, or simply laughing at the absurdity, remember: bullshit is temporary, but your integrity is permanent.

Leaders come and go, but your ability to see through the noise and thrive despite it is a skill that will serve you in any workplace. So, the next time your boss declares, "We're redefining the future of innovation," smile politely, nod strategically, and quietly think: "Sure, Jan." Then, return to the work that matters because you've got this.

Leadership often involves a mix of inspiration and nonsense, ranging from harmless exaggerations to manipulative rhetoric. While some leaders use embellished stories to motivate and uplift, others exploit emotions with empty promises and buzzwords to mask a lack of substance. The key is discerning whether the leader's style energizes or confuses the team. Inspirational nonsense motivates employees, while manipulative rhetoric often results in skepticism and disengagement.

To navigate a leader prone to bullshit, identify red flags like overuse of jargon, lack of accountability, relentless positivity that ignores reality, and repeated empty promises. When addressing these issues, focus on ideas rather than individuals, use questions to expose gaps, and choose private settings for constructive feedback. If calling out nonsense isn't an option, ground yourself in your values, translate rhetoric into actionable tasks, and find humor in the absurdity. By focusing on the bigger picture and maintaining your integrity, you can thrive even under a leader prone to polished nonsense.

CHAPTER 30

HOLLYWOOD BULLSHIT

Hollywood is the glittering epicenter of creative nonsense, where reality is bent, stretched, and ignored to deliver stories that entertain, inspire, and occasionally leave us scratching our heads. From "based on a true story" claims riddled with fiction to character arcs that defy logic and physics, Hollywood has mastered the art of smoke and mirrors. And here's the twist: we love it. Let's explore the cinematic land of exaggerated truths improbable transformations, and why we keep returning for more.

THE "BASED ON A TRUE STORY" TRAP

A few phrases captivate audiences, such as "based on a true story." It's Hollywood's way of saying, "This might've happened if you squint." These words lend even the wildest narratives a sheen of credibility, convincing us we're watching history unfold, albeit with more explosions and better lighting.

Take the Texas Chainsaw Massacre, a film marketed as real-life horror. The so-called "true story" was loosely inspired by Ed Gain, a criminal with macabre hobbies, but Leatherface and his chainsaw? Pure invention. The Audience didn't care. The actual story label made it all the more terrifying, even as the facts fell apart.

Even movies with some basis in reality, like The Social Network, aren't immune to Hollywood embellishments. Sure, Mark Zuckerberg founded Facebook, but the snappy dialogue and dramatic confrontations? Likely more Aaron Sorkin than reality. Yet, we embrace these dramatizations because watching someone quietly code in a dorm room doesn't exactly scream box office gold.

The truth is audiences crave truthy stories more than the truth itself. We want the drama, the stakes, and the emotional highs, even if it means sacrificing accuracy. Hollywood knows this, and the "based on a true story" tagline has become less about authenticity and more about creating permission to escape into a polished version of reality.

UNREALISTIC CHARACTER ARCS: FROM ZERO TO HERO IN 90 MINUTES

In Hollywood, character transformations happen at warp speed. While real-life change is slow and messy, on-screen growth is swift, dramatic, and often soundtracked by an inspiring montage. One moment, the protagonist is a bumbling nobody; the next, they're scaling impossible heights, literally or metaphorically.

Consider Rocky, where a down-on-his-luck boxer becomes a heavyweight contender seemingly overnight. The training montages, set to Bill Conti's iconic "Gonna Fly Now," make us believe that anything is possible with enough grit (and music). While undeniably inspiring, it also sets a bar so high it's almost comical. Real life doesn't have dramatic crescendos to push us through grueling workouts.

Romantic comedies offer their own brand of implausibility. The "plain Jane" trope is a repeat offender cue the moment when the lead removes their glasses and lets their hair down, instantly transforming into the room's most captivating person. This wouldn't make you unrecognizable; it might just make your hairstyle more aerodynamic.

Despite their absurdity, these character arcs resonate because they tap into universal desires for self-improvement and redemption. Hollywood condenses a lifetime's worth of growth into two hours, giving us hope that change is possible if not quite so cinematic in execution.

WHY WE LOVE TO SUSPEND DISBELIEF

Hollywood thrives on our willingness to suspend disbelief. Deep down, we know dinosaurs can't be resurrected, cars don't morph into robots, and Tom Cruise isn't actually scaling skyscrapers without a safety net. Yet, we eagerly embrace these fantasies because they offer what reality often lacks: excitement, escape, and a sense of wonder.

This suspension of disbelief is an unspoken agreement between filmmakers and audiences. We overlook glaring plot holes and absurd scenarios in exchange for entertainment. It's why no one questions how James Bond's tuxedo stays immaculate through explosions or why superhero costumes remain spotless after battles.

At its core, our love for Hollywood's nonsense is rooted in our love of storytelling. For millennia, humans have crafted tales that stretch reality. Hollywood added CGI, big budgets, and A-list stars. These stories let us explore the impossible, grapple with moral dilemmas, and experience emotions on a grander scale.

There's also an element of wish fulfillment. Hollywood's flights of fancy let us believe that the impossible is possible, that underdogs can triumph, impossible heists can succeed, and superheroes can save the day. It's not about reality; it's about possibility.

WHEN BULLSHIT ENHANCES STORYTELLING

Not all Hollywood nonsense is created equal. When used thoughtfully, it can elevate a story, adding depth and emotional resonance. The Lord of the Rings may have talking trees and magical rings. Still, its fantastical elements highlight universal themes like friendship, sacrifice, and power. The bullshit isn't distracting, it's integral.

Similarly, films like Interstellar push the limits of believability to explore profound questions about time, love, and humanity's survival. The science may leave experts scratching, but the story's emotional impact is undeniable.

Even unapologetically over-the-top franchises like The Fast and the Furious know how to use nonsense to their advantage. The gravity-defying stunts and absurd plot twists aren't trying to be realistic; they're delivering pure, unfiltered escapism. The audience knows what they've signed up for: cars, chaos, and Vin Diesel growling about family.

The key is balance. When used sparingly and with purpose, Hollywood bullshit amplifies storytelling. Overdone, it risks alienating audiences (cough, Cats). The best filmmakers understand this balance, crafting narratives that feel larger than life without completely abandoning logic or at least making us care enough not to notice.

EMBRACING HOLLYWOOD'S NONSENSE

Hollywood's magic lies in its ability to make us believe in the unbelievable. Whether it's exaggerating true stories, crafting implausible character arcs, or creating entirely fantastical worlds, the industry excels at selling dreams wrapped in a touch of nonsense. And we, the audience, are more than happy to buy in.

At its best, Hollywood bullshit isn't about deceiving it's about inspiring. It reminds us that while real life might lack montages and guaranteed happy endings, it's still full of possibilities. So, lean in the next time you find yourself rolling your eyes at a movie's absurdity. Suspend disbelief, embrace the fantasy, and let Hollywood take you on a ride. After all, in this world of endless possibilities, even the impossible becomes a little more believable.

Hollywood thrives on bending reality to create entertaining, inspiring and sometimes absurd stories. From "based on a true story" taglines that stretch facts to character arcs that defy logic, the industry has mastered the art of smoke and mirrors. Audiences love these exaggerations, embracing polished narratives over mundane realities because they offer drama, stakes, and emotional highs.

KEY EXAMPLES OF HOLLYWOOD NONSENSE

"Based on a True Story": Films often exaggerate real events for dramatic impact, like The Texas Chainsaw Massacre and The Social Network, where facts take a backseat to storytelling flair.

Unrealistic Transformations: Movies like Rocky and romantic comedies compress lifelong growth into montages and instant makeovers, appealing to universal desires for self-improvement and redemption.

Suspension of Disbelief: Audiences accept improbable scenarios from dinosaurs in Jurassic Park to gravity-defying stunts in The Fast and the Furious in exchange for excitement, escape, and wonder.

When done right, Hollywood's nonsense elevates storytelling, creating emotional resonance and exploring universal themes like friendship, sacrifice, and hope. However, the key lies in balance; too much absurdity risks alienating audiences.

Ultimately, Hollywood's magic inspires us to believe in the impossible. By embracing its creative embellishments, we're reminded that while real life may lack cinematic montages, it's still filled with potential for extraordinary moments.

CHAPTER 31

MARKETING MYTHS

If you've ever looked at an ad and thought, "That's too good to be true," you're on the right track. Marketing thrives on exaggeration, crafting aspirational fantasies that blur the line between reality and wishful thinking. With Photoshopped perfection, exaggerated claims, and taglines catchy enough to sell ice to penguins, advertisers have perfected the art of creative nonsense. Let's explore the tall tales of marketing, why we fall for them, and how to see through the smoke and mirrors without losing our sense of humor.

THE TALL TALES OF AD CAMPAIGNS

Marketing is a master of hyperbole, serving promises that are often more fiction than fact. Take Red Bull's iconic tagline, "Red Bull gives you wings." It was clever and unforgettable but also wildly untrue. The company even settled a lawsuit after customers argued they felt no metaphorical or literal lift after drinking the energy beverage. The message wasn't about functionality; it was about selling a feeling of limitless energy.

The beauty industry is no stranger to these tactics. Mascara ads boast "300% more volume" without ever defining what that percentage means. Look closer, and you'll spot disclaimers like "lashes enhanced with inserts." Translation? The model's lashes are fakes, so your results will be, at best, underwhelming.

Then there's the fitness and diet industry, purveyors of the "too good to be true" fantasy. Vibrating ab machines promise chiseled physiques in just five minutes daily, but most users only gain regret. These campaigns prey on our desire for shortcuts, offering solutions wrapped in sleek packaging but delivering little more than empty promises.

The genius of these campaigns is that they don't just sell products; they sell aspirations. Whether it's energy, beauty, or fitness, the ads promise transformation. The product becomes secondary to the lifestyle it represents, pulling us into a fantasy we're all too eager to buy.

WHY WE FALL FOR THE NONSENSE

Despite knowing better, we often fall for marketing myths. Why? Because humans are emotional creatures, and advertising is designed to manipulate our feelings.

Nostalgia is one of marketers' most potent tools. Think back to cereal commercials where a single bite turned kids into superheroes. We knew the sugary flakes wouldn't grant powers, but the magic sold us. Even as adults, nostalgia taps into that longing for simpler, more exciting times, making brands like Coca-Cola and Disney masters of emotional persuasion.

Scarcity is another clever trick. Phrases like "Limited time only!" or "While supplies last!" make us panic that we'll miss out on a rare opportunity. The urgency is artificial. Those sneakers will likely appear at a discount next season, but at the moment, it feels like it will be now or never.

Social proof is equally effective. A product labeled "America's #1 choice" or "Loved by millions" taps into our herd mentality. If everyone else loves it, it must be worth trying, right? Often, these claims are based on vague or questionable data, but the implied popularity is enough to sway us.

Ultimately, ads succeed because they appeal to our emotions, nostalgia, fear of missing out, and desire to belong, leaving logic in the dust.

SPOTTING THE MARKETING MYTHS

The good news? You don't need a PhD in advertising to spot the nonsense. A little skepticism and attention to detail go a long way.

READ THE FINE PRINT

Those tiny disclaimers at the bottom of ads reveal everything marketers don't want you to notice. Phrases like "Results not typical" or "Not intended to diagnose or treat" are dead giveaways that the promises are more fantasy than fact.

QUESTION THE NUMBERS

When a product boasts "95% effective," ask yourself: effective at what? Numbers can be manipulated to sound impressive, so don't accept them at face value.

IDENTIFY THE EMOTIONAL HOOK

Good advertising sells feelings, not facts. If an ad stirs nostalgia, confidence, or even insecurity, you've found the hook. Recognizing this can help you step back and think critically.

DO YOUR RESEARCH

The internet is your best friend. Before spending big on a "miracle" product, read reviews from real customers. If the feedback includes phrases like "smelled weird" or "did nothing," save your money.

EMBRACING HUMOR AND SKEPTICISM

The best way to approach marketing myths is with humor and critical thinking. Instead of feeling duped, laugh at the absurdity. That face cream promising to make you look 10 years younger? Smile, shake your head, and move on. Ads featuring dramatic perfume commercials where everyone's inexplicably running through a desert? Pure comedy gold.

Not all marketing is bad. Some brands genuinely deliver on their promises. The key is separating honest advertising from empty exaggerations. By maintaining a critical eye, you can enjoy the creativity of advertising without falling for the nonsense.

WHY WE KEEP BUYING (AND THAT'S OKAY)

Even the savviest among us occasionally fall for clever ads. Whether it's the catchy slogan, sleek design, or a moment of weakness during an Instagram scroll, marketing sometimes wins. And that's okay.

The trick is balance. Splurge on the fancy moisturizer if it makes you feel good, but don't expect miracles. Buy the high-tech blender for your smoothie obsession, but know it won't make kale taste like chocolate cake. Enjoy the fantasy without losing sight of reality.

At its heart, marketing is storytelling with a sales pitch. It's up to us to decide which stories we believe and which we laugh off.

MARKETING MYTHS AS ENTERTAINMENT

Marketing myths will always exist; they're the bread and butter of advertising. But that doesn't mean we have to fall for them. By approaching ads with curiosity, skepticism, and a sense of humor, we can enjoy their creativity without letting them manipulate us.

So, the next time you see an ad promising to change your life, chuckle, raise an eyebrow, and move on. In a world of marketing myths, the greatest power lies in your ability to think critically and laugh freely. Cheers to being gloriously skeptical!

SUMMARY

Marketing thrives on crafting aspirational fantasies that blur the line between reality and fiction. Ads like "Red Bull gives you wings" or mascara boasting "300% more volume" sell emotions, not facts, by tapping into desires for confidence, nostalgia, and belonging. They use clever tactics like exaggerated claims, scarcity-driven urgency ("Limited time only!"), and social proof to manipulate emotions and encourage purchases. The fitness and beauty industries are prime culprits, promising miraculous transformations with little substance. While the allure of these ads lies in their creativity and storytelling, they often leave consumers chasing unattainable ideals.

A healthy mix of humor and skepticism is key to navigating marketing myths. Reading the fine print, questioning vague statistics, and identifying emotional hooks can help separate fact from fiction. While indulging in occasional splurges for joy or convenience is okay, managing expectations and selling feelings is important not guaranteed. By critically evaluating claims and laughing at the absurdity of over-the-top campaigns, consumers can enjoy the entertainment value of advertising without falling for its nonsense. The most significant power lies in thinking critically and staying grounded amidst the allure of polished promises.

CHAPTER 32

BULLSHIT AND THE POST-TRUTH ERA

Welcome to the post-Truth Era, a world where feelings overpower facts and reality becomes whatever resonates most loudly. In this environment, emotions take precedence over evidence, allowing bullshit to flourish as the dominant form of communication. It's both fascinating and unsettling, as perception increasingly outweighs reality. Let's delve into how we arrived here, why emotional narratives dominate, and how to navigate a world where truth often takes a backseat to convenience.

FEELINGS OVER FACTS: THE RISE OF EMOTIONAL TRUTH

Once, facts were the bedrock of reasoned discourse, unassailable as long as evidence supported them. But in today's landscape, emotional resonance often overrides logical rigor. The phrase "I feel like…" has become a cornerstone of modern rhetoric, placing subjective experiences on par with objective truths.

Why do emotions hold such sway? They're universal, immediate, and deeply engaging. A compelling anecdote outshines a dense data spreadsheet because stories evoke empathy and connect with our humanity. Politicians and marketers know this all too well, crafting narratives that appeal to our hearts rather than our heads.

Social media amplifies this trend, rewarding emotionally charged content with likes, shares, and comments. Outrage, joy, and fear generate engagement, creating an ecosystem where sensationalism thrives. In this emotionally driven culture, nuanced, fact-based discussions struggle to gain traction. Instead, we gravitate toward memes and headlines that validate our feelings, even if they stretch the truth or obliterate it entirely.

The danger lies in how easily this dynamic fuels misinformation. Emotionally satisfying falsehoods spread faster than uncomfortable truths, creating an environment where half-truths and outright fabrications are accepted and celebrated. Once bullshit gains momentum, reeling it back becomes almost impossible.

THE ECHO CHAMBER EFFECT

Echo chambers, self-reinforcing bubbles where everyone agrees with you, are one of the most insidious consequences of the post-truth era. These digital sanctuaries validate beliefs, regardless of their accuracy, and shield participants from contradictory perspectives.

Within echo chambers, even the most absurd ideas can flourish. Flat Earth theories, vaccine microchip conspiracies, and claims of time-traveling lizard overlords gain traction because these spaces provide unwavering support. Belonging often outweighs the discomfort of questioning one's beliefs, creating a fertile ground for nonsense to take root and thrive.

But echo chambers aren't just for fringe groups. Social media algorithms curate our feeds to show us content we're likely to engage with, creating tailored realities that reinforce our existing views. Over time, this narrows our perspective, making any challenge to our beliefs feel like an attack.

Escaping these bubbles requires deliberate effort. Seeking opposing viewpoints and engaging with them thoughtfully can broaden your understanding and sharpen your ability to discern truth. It's not easy or comfortable, but it's essential for breaking free from the cycle of validation and misinformation.

WHY PERCEPTION OUTWEIGHS REALITY

In the post-truth world, perception trumps facts. A statement doesn't need to be accurate to be powerful. It just needs to be believable or emotionally resonant. This simplicity makes perception so effective; it reduces complex issues to digestible sound bites that feel satisfying, even if they're misleading.

Take celebrity endorsements. Do we really believe an athlete's success stems from a particular cereal brand? Of course not. However, the perception of greatness linked to the product is enough to drive sales. Similarly, political slogans like "Hope and Change" or "Make America Great Again" succeed because they evoke feelings and aspirations rather than presenting detailed policies.

This reliance on perception creates a culture where bullshit isn't just accepted; it's expected. Complex truths are replaced by oversimplified narratives, and they stick as long as they feel good.

PROMOTING TRUTH IN A POST-TRUTH WORLD

How do we push back against the rise of bullshit without denying the emotional power of storytelling? The key lies in balancing feelings with facts, encouraging critical thinking, and fostering a culture of curiosity.

- **Be Curious, Not Combative**

  Approach differing opinions with a mindset of inquiry. Ask questions and seek evidence instead of immediately dismissing opposing viewpoints. Respectful dialogue can illuminate truth more effectively than heated debates.

- **Fact-Check Before You Share**

  In the age of instant sharing, take a moment to verify the accuracy of what resonates with you. A quick fact-check can prevent the spread of misinformation and protect your credibility.

- **Encourage Critical Thinking**

  Teach yourself and others to question sensational headlines and viral claims. Critical thinking is a powerful antidote to bullshit, helping you navigate complex issues with clarity.

- **Amplify Reliable Sources**

  Support evidence-based journalism and science. Sharing their work helps counter the noise of misinformation and reinforces the value of factual accuracy.

- **Embrace Nuance**

    Truth rarely fits into neat categories. Accepting complexity and resisting oversimplified narratives can lead to a deeper understanding of the world.

    Promoting truth in the post-truth era isn't about rejecting emotion but ensuring that feelings don't overshadow facts.

- **Navigating the Bullshit Storm**

    The post-truth era is rife with emotional appeals, echo chambers, and the triumph of perception over reality. Yet, it also presents an opportunity to rise above the noise by cultivating curiosity, critical thinking, and skepticism.

    So, the next time someone says, "I feel like this is true," pause and respond with, "That's interesting. What evidence supports it?" It may not win you instant popularity, but it will anchor you in reality, and that's a victory worth celebrating.

THE FINAL BS BREAKDOWN

So here we are. After a whirlwind tour through the wild and wonderful world of bullshit, it's time to step back, take a deep breath, and assess what we've learned. From spotting the nonsense to wielding it responsibly, this book has been your guide to navigating a world where BS is both an art form and an epidemic.

What's the big takeaway? BS is everywhere, and, like it or not, it's part of being human. But the key to thriving in this nonsense-filled world is learning to spot it, manage it, and, when necessary, call it out (or add a sprinkle of your own). Let's take a moment to revisit the biggest lessons we've covered and distill them into a practical guide for living in harmony with the BS around us.

Bullshit is everywhere, often hiding in plain sight behind confidence, buzzwords, or a perfectly curated social media post. Recognizing it is the first step in navigating this maze of nonsense. Watch for red flags like overconfidence, suspiciously specific details, or clichés that seem too good to be true. Trust your instincts; if something feels off, it probably is. A simple follow-up question like, "Tell me more about that," can unravel even the most polished façade. Once identified, not every piece of BS requires your energy—some nonsense is harmless, while other lies can be harmful. Picking your battles is key: let entertaining nonsense slide, diffuse the ridiculous with humor, or gracefully walk away when it's not worth it.

When BS crosses the line into destructive territory, calling it out becomes necessary, but it doesn't have to be confrontational. Approach it with curiosity questions like "How did that work?" and keep the tone light while encouraging clarity. A dash of humor softens the blow, and knowing when to stop prevents unnecessary conflict. On the flip side, not all BS is bad; used thoughtfully, it can smooth over awkward situations, bring humor to a dull moment, or help build connections. Ethical BS is about kindness and levity, whether you're complimenting someone's less-than-perfect karaoke skills or inventing a playful family legend. The key is to enhance social interactions without undermining trust.

In a digital age supercharged with nonsense, detoxing from BS can be a refreshing reset. Take breaks from the curated perfection of social media, embrace authenticity, and recalibrate your tolerance for fluff. A

BS detox isn't about erasing it from your life but resetting your balance. Learn to wield bullshit thoughtfully, adding charm without manipulation, humor without harm, and truth without unnecessary bluntness. After all, life's a circus, and mastering the art of navigating its nonsense keeps it interesting.

THE GRAND TAKEAWAY

BS is like salt. It's everywhere, and a little goes a long way. Too much ruins the dish, but the right amount can enhance the flavor. This book isn't about eradicating BS (good luck with that) but mastering it. By recognizing, dodging, and wielding it responsibly, you can navigate life's nonsense with humor, grace, and a clear conscience.

So, here's the final nugget of wisdom: Life's a circus, and BS is the juggling act. Sometimes, you're dodging it, throwing it, but most of the time, you're just trying not to trip over it. Laugh at the absurdity, embrace the lessons, and remember: the best thing you can do in a world full of nonsense is keep your balance and sense of humor.

Now, master the art of BS and make the world less serious and fun. After all, if you can't beat the bullshit, you might as well enjoy the ride.

The post-Truth Era is defined by emotions overriding facts, where perception often outweighs reality. Emotional narratives resonate more powerfully than data-driven arguments, allowing misinformation to thrive. Social media amplifies this phenomenon, rewarding sensational content with likes and shares while marginalizing nuanced, evidence-based discussions. Echo chambers reinforce biases, creating self-validating bubbles that isolate people from contradictory viewpoints. In this environment, emotionally satisfying falsehoods often spread faster than uncomfortable truths, fostering an ecosystem where bullshit is not only accepted but celebrated.

Fostering critical thinking, curiosity, and skepticism is essential to combat this trend. Strategies include fact-checking, seeking diverse perspectives, and promoting evidence-based sources. While emotions are powerful tools for engagement, balancing them with facts ensures thoughtful discourse and reduces the spread of misinformation. By questioning claims and embracing nuance, individuals can navigate the storm of modern bullshit, ensuring that their decisions are informed by truth rather than convenience. The key to thriving in this era lies in balancing emotional appeal with intellectual rigor and a commitment to seeking the facts.

This book masterfully dissects the pervasive presence of bullshit across various aspects of life, offering a humorous yet incisive lens through which to navigate its many forms. From corporate buzzwords to Hollywood exaggerations, romantic white lies, and social media illusions, the book exposes how nonsense has woven itself into the fabric of modern existence. At its core, the text reveals that bullshit is both a coping mechanism and a tool for manipulation, thriving on human emotions, social pressures, and the increasingly blurred lines between reality and perception.

One of the book's central themes is the balance between bullshit's harmless charm and its potential to erode trust. It acknowledges that some nonsense can bring levity to relationships, creativity to leadership, and flair to storytelling. However, when wielded irresponsibly, bullshit can fuel misinformation, foster distrust, and create toxic environments. Through vivid examples and relatable anecdotes, the chapters invite readers to recognize this duality and approach bullshit with discernment and humor.

Another highlight is the book's exploration of how emotional narratives often overpower facts, especially in the post-truth era. It critiques how algorithms, echo chambers, and sensationalism exacerbate this trend, turning bullshit into an unstoppable force in media, marketing, and everyday communication. Yet, the book remains optimistic, providing actionable strategies for cutting through the noise, fostering authenticity, and cultivating critical thinking.

Ultimately, the book serves as both a guide and a call to action, encouraging readers to navigate life's nonsense with grace, integrity, and skepticism. By understanding and mastering the art of bullshit, whether to identify, challenge, or strategically use it, we can better connect with others, enhance our resilience, and find meaning amid the absurdities of modern life.

www.ingramcontent.com/pod-product-compliance
Lightning Source LLC
Chambersburg PA
CBHW050252010526
44107CB00003B/290